Advance Praise

"This book is monumental and speaks to anyone who is no longer happy in their medical career. Thank you for being the voice for thousands who need you!"

Shawna Purcell, MD
Director and founder of PurcellMDical
Author of Fat Loss. Diabetes
Control. Longevity Health.

"I am in awe and in tears after reading this book. It's absolutely wonderful, with stories and fables woven in and out, and filled with scientific wisdom and the best coaching paradigms that help to explain that wisdom. This book is and will be an inspiration to all, not only to those who seek new ways to serve in the world and live their purpose, but also for those who need to see how envisioning their life through a new lens can enhance their own wellbeing. Dr. Zhong has done a phenomenal job writing this life and soul-saving book. It is a gift to the human race."

Ceseli Milstein, RN, BS, MA
Certified Transformational Coach
Founder of cOMe hOMe to OM Health
and Wellness Coaching

"Embarking on a new journey to change the status quo is a challenge. It requires deep consideration of life values and passionate pursuit of becoming the best possible you. In this book, Xuemei bravely describes her personal quest and provides poignant questions for reflection while distilling the experience for others who are at a crossroads in their biomedical career. Those who wish to have a positive impact on the people they meet and the world around them can find new hope and motivation in Xuemei's words."

Tamar Aprahamian Putiri, PhD
Founder and principal,
JetPub Scientific Communications

"Burnout among medical professionals is extremely high due to patient demand/overload, lack of support within the medical system, and lack of good personal care. Add to that a sense of "well I must keep going because I went through medical/advanced schooling and it's my path" and "I'm strong, I have to suck it up, and just work harder." This is the mindset that many follow instead of shifting how they live and work or follow their career path. The idea that "there must be something wrong with me that I am burnt out" leads to more burnout, a sense of feeling trapped and helpless, and perpetual unhappiness and unhealthiness. Honestly looking at ourselves and addressing burnout first and foremost is key. Dr. Zhong writes with wisdom and from her heart, providing easy-to-follow strategies to shift your career and create the life you're meant to live. This book will help you to find the courage and to leverage your gifts to do what's aligned with your true self and your path."

Denise Morett, *Doctor of Psychology*
Professor at Vassar College
Bestselling author of Lifeline

"If you are struggling with making a big change in your career, this book is perfect for you. If you are not happy with your current work and, also worried about what is on the other side, this book will empower you to move in the direction of experiencing peace and joy in your career!"

Teri Yunus, *NP & Whole Health Coach*
Founder of Health Up with Teri Health
& Wellness Coaching LLC

The Joy of Letting Go
of Your Biomedical Career

The Joy of
Letting Go OF YOUR
BIOMEDICAL
CAREER

The Ultimate Quitter's Guide
to Flourish *Without the Burnout*

DR. XUEMEI ZHONG

NEW YORK

LONDON • NASHVILLE • MELBOURNE • VANCOUVER

The Joy of Letting Go of Your Biomedical Career

The Ultimate Quitter's Guide to Flourish Without the Burnout

Published in New York, New York, by Morgan James Publishing in partnership with Difference Press. Morgan James is a trademark of Morgan James, LLC. www.MorganJamesPublishing.com

ISBN 9781642798821 paperback
ISBN 9781642798838 eBook
Library of Congress Control Number: 2019952546

Cover Design Concept: Jennifer Stimson

Cover & Interior Design: Chris Treccani   www.3dogcreative.net

Editor: Todd Hunter

Book Coaching: The Author Incubator

Author Photo: The Image Group

Morgan James is a proud partner of Habitat for Humanity Peninsula and Greater Williamsburg. Partners in building since 2006.

Get involved today! Visit
MorganJamesPublishing.com/giving-back

To all my mentors who saw my potential
and believed in me.

To all my fellow coaches who encouraged me
when I needed it the most.

To my parents who gave me the gift of
teaching and mentoring.

To my husband who supported me all the way.

To my dearest children who always gave me
the first and honest critiques.

To my readers who gave me purpose.

Table of Contents

Introduction   xiii

Part 1   **My Journey**   **1**
Chapter 1   My Parents Were Proud of Me,
              But I Was Suffering...   3
Chapter 2   Ending My Double Life   15
Chapter 3   Ask and You Shall Receive   29

Part 2   **The 7-Step UPLEVEL Process**   **45**
Chapter 4   Step 1: U for Unload   47
              (Unload the Problem, Sitting Back,
              and Watch the Movie)
Chapter 5   Step 2: P for Purpose   59
              (Reclaim Your Purpose)
Chapter 6   Step 3: L for Leverage   73
              (Leverage Your Gift and Turn Quitting
              into Upgrading)
Chapter 7   Step 4: E for Envision   87
              (Build Your Unique Vision, and Say,
              "Yes, I Am Coming.")

Chapter 8   Step 5: V for Voice   97
             (Removing Roadblocks by Giving the
             Parts of Internal Conflicts Their Voices)
Chapter 9   Step 6: E for Empower   105
             (Take Only Empowered Action)
Chapter 10   Step 7: L for Level   117
             (Level a New Career Path by Passing
             the Stress Test)

Part 3   Proceed with Inevitable Success   131
Chapter 11   Why Most People Either Can't Make the
             Decision or Regret the Decision Later   133
Chapter 12   What Is Your Life Mission Statement?   143

Afterword   151
Acknowledgements   153
Thank You for Reading My Book   155
Other Books by Dr. Zhong   156
About the Author   159

Introduction

In 2011, I visited the Great Vermont Maze on our family vacation. The maze covers 24 acres of land with trails lined with walls of ten-foot-tall corn stalks. Every year, the maze has a different design. That year, it was a Falcon. It is said that most people underestimate the challenge, and 90% of teenagers give up in less than twenty minutes and have little interest in really solving the maze. It usually takes two to three hours to solve the maze. I was with my nine-year-old son and six-year-old daughter. It was a hot summer afternoon. After an hour or so, the kids were getting bored and tired. When the sun started to set, I was wondering if we were ever going to get out. Luckily, there were shortcuts, emergency exits on the map. There were also a few bridges where you could climb high enough to have an aerial view of the maze and get a big picture of where you were. More interestingly, we found couple of large "panic" bells you could strike for help. The staff would come to "rescue" you when they heard the bells.

After more than a decade of graduate school and postdoctoral fellowship training, I finally became a junior faculty at the Boston University School of Medicine. I enthusiastically dived into the maze of the biomedical research field only to realize there was no emergency exit. I thought I would study and admire the human immune system and inspire my students to pursue biomedical science. But soon, I found I was doing less and less research and mentoring. More and more, I was buried in endless research grant applications, manuscript writing, resubmission, and writing all kinds of protocols and safety trainings. To make matters worse, I had to surrender my innovative ideas and concepts to projects that investors would see profitable or translational. After losing my father and my mentor to cancer and seeing my brilliant colleagues, students, and technicians suffer from tremendous pressure and work-life imbalance, I wanted to get out of the maze. But there is no emergency exit and no guidance. Ph.D. and M.D. students have been trained to be resilient, to sacrifice our lives, and to compete in order to rise to the top. We were raised to honor perseverance and not giving up. We were supported for all of that. But we were not trained nor supported on how to let go, how to self-care, how to upgrade, how to create. I struggled to find my new path that was more fulfilling and in alignment of my original dream. I knew I didn't want to stay like that for the rest of my career. I knew my gift and full potential were not used and would be wasted if I kept burying myself in the soul-sucking grant, manuscript, and administrative paperwork. But what else could I do? How could I get out? How could I help people more without losing my own life? I wished there were guidance and some handholding at times when I needed it the most.

With the rise of burnout, stress, and depression for both clinical and research staffs, more and more people are expressing concerns such as:

- Should I quit my medical career?

- Is medical school worth leaving?
- I want out, but I still owe so much in student loans.
- I feel burnout while in the hospital system but alive when I volunteer outside. What's going on?
- What are the viable alternative career options for M.D. Ph. D.?
- So much career advice out there. Which one to take? How do I know that will be better and worth the risk of quitting my current job?

There is a lot of advice out there on how to deal with burnout but most of them aren't really sustainable. There is a lot of career advice on the Internet. But not many realize this is not just about finding another job. It is my hope that this book will provide the ultimate holistic tools for a safe and glorious exit especially for professionals in the biomedical field. If you follow the steps, by the time you finish reading this book, you will have an executable plan for an inevitably successful and fulfilling career.

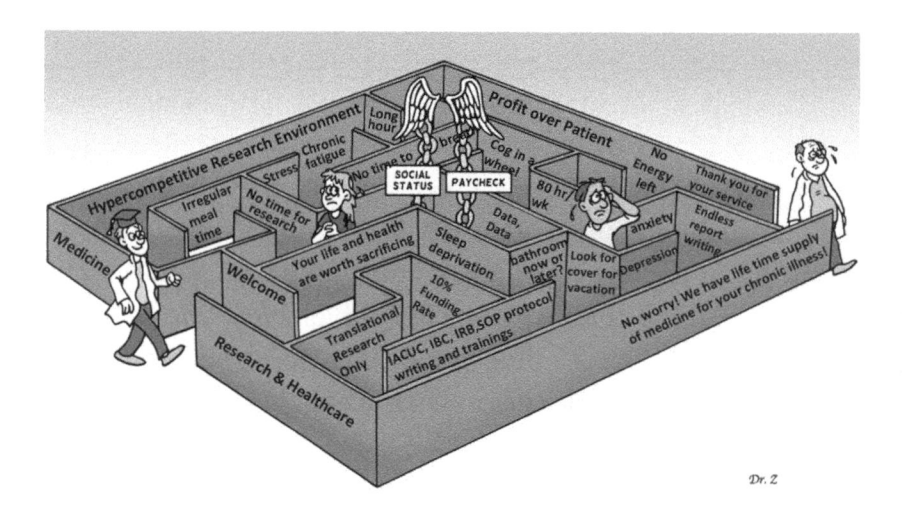

Part 1

My Journey

Chapter 1

My Parents Were Proud of Me, But I Was Suffering...

My Parents Want the Best for Me

was mad at my dad. It was late in the night. I was watching a famous Japanese TV series about a group of schoolgirls on a volleyball team. Like other teenage girls in China at that time, I became a big fan of that TV series and dreamed of becoming a volleyball player. That was probably the time when the Chinese volleyball team started rising to the world championship. Almost every schoolgirl started to play volleyball because of this TV series and it became a nationwide sport, even surpassing Ping-Pong. You can imagine how much I wanted to finish that episode when my dad came in and brutally turned off the TV. I felt he was the worst dad in the world and thought I would never forgive him. Of course, he just wanted me to go to sleep early so I could go back to school.

My middle school was a boarding school that was a two-hour bus ride away. We didn't have cars back then. There was a middle school only minutes away from home. But that was not a good enough one for me. I am an only child and my parents wanted the best for me. There was a shuttle bus taking us back to school every Sunday evening. But when I was sick and needed to get back to school in the middle of the week, my dad would bike for an hour with me sitting on the back rack with all my heavy books, food, and clothes in my backpack. It was a long unpaved country road. Under other circumstances, it would take a couple of buses to get to school. At that time, there were no world-class subways in that area like there are today. But my parents were worried that I would get lost or kidnapped as a little girl while walking to different bus stations. So my dad would bike a long way and drop me off at the bus stop of the last leg of bus trip so I could get off right in front of my school with just one bus to take.

It was always a pleasant ride with the beautiful countryside. I looked forward to getting to school with all the goodies packed by my mom. I never realized how hard my dad had to peddle the bike with my heavy backpack and me. His pants were full of sweat by the time he dropped me off and he'd still have to bike another hour back home. He never complained and was always happy to wave goodbye to me.

To my parents, having good grades at school, going to a good college, and having a good job were all they wanted for me. And I made them proud of me when I graduated from college being the first double-majored student at the university. My story was written in the history book of the university. I made my parents proud again when after graduation, I entered the Chinese Academy of Science, the top biochemistry research institute, after graduation. But that was not enough. In the late 80s and early 90s, what could really make your parents proud was going to America to study. Unlike these days, where many Chinese families can afford sending their kids to US, at that time, most Chinese families could not afford that. The only way to go to the US was to apply for scholarships that required a strong academic background. Therefore, if your child could go to the US to study, it usually meant he or she was really good. That became my dream. I didn't realize back then, being approved and praised by my parents was the main drive of my life. I studied hard and got top GRE and TOFEL scores and finally got accepted by the Molecular and Biotechnology masters program at University of Massachusetts at Boston. At that time, not many people knew universities in the US. Some relatives thought I was going to MIT. That made my parents super proud. They didn't really want to correct them. But they could not tell anyway. But if I would've gone to Harvard or MIT, that would've really made my parents proud. I studied hard and graduated with honors in two years. That was the first time my parents were officially invited to come to the US and attend my graduation ceremony.

My parents were super happy for the trip. My dad took hundreds of pictures detailing everything from preparing for the trip at the airport, all the way to my apartment, and my first car I used to drive around my parents. At that time, there were no digital cameras. Imagine how many rolls of film had to be developed. His excitement and pride were written on his face and he recorded it on those photos forever. But one moment he regretted the most, was when I went onto the stage to accept my student research achievement award from the president. My dad was so proud that his hands trembled and he missed that moment and only took a blurry picture of me walking down the stage. My mission of making my parents proud of me didn't stop there. After graduation, I got accepted into the Immunology PhD program at Boston University School of Medicine with the prestigious President Scholarship. Before school started, I took my parents to visit the main campus along the Charles River across Harvard and MIT and I bought them a BU t-shirt that says "All those who cannot go to BU go to Harvard." I was happy that they were proud of me. When my dad went back to Shanghai, he wrote an article about the whole experience of attending my graduation ceremony, traveling around the New England area, and sending me to Boston University School of Medicine. That article was published in the local newspaper.

After starting my Ph.D. program, I began to study and work 24/7 and had less and less time to call or write letters to my parents. At that time, they didn't have computers and couldn't email from home.

My busy schedule however served as a perfect excuse at that time. I felt less and less sure of what I could talk to them about. All our conversations were about eating well, keeping warm, and sleeping tight. The rest of the conversation was complaining about each other. My parents' marriage was probably in trouble from the day they married. I didn't remember a week in my life that they didn't have some sort of argument. The arguments ranged from as small as how to squeeze the toothpaste tube, wipe the table, or hang the clothes, to as big as how to raise me, to politics and how the world should be. They both loved me in very different ways but they had to fight about it. It was never violent. But it hurt. Going to the US was a perfect way to escape from their drama. I didn't even want to hear their argument around my marriage. My mother had high hopes. She thought I was a princess and must marry a prince and really didn't like my boyfriend and his family. We kind of eloped and got married in Hawaii without parents. Even though we went back afterward to China where both our families prepared wedding banquets for us, I really liked getting married without my parents. I still wanted them to be proud of me as if that could save their marriage. So my mission continued. After five years of hard work, I graduated. This time, there was much more to celebrate as I gave birth to my first child a month after my graduation. My parents came to my commencement watching me hooded by my mentor on the stage. A few weeks later, they were holding their first grandchild. Parties, flowers, and congratulations filled the memories captured by photos. But behind all the excitement, the almost daily arguments continued. One of the heated debates was vegetarianism. As both my husband and I became vegetarian, what to feed our baby became the center of all the fights between me and my parents. They thought vegetarianism was superstitious and non-scientific, and that we must be brainwashed by some cult.

My parents were proud of me and my husband when we became medical school professors at Boston University and Harvard University. If they could, they would proudly tell everyone in the world. But they would never tell a soul that we were vegetarians and seeking truth beyond the science that they knew. My mission of making my parents proud and saving their marriage started to fall apart when my father one day wanted to talk to me alone. He asked my permission to divorce my mom and marry someone else. Tired of fighting with my mom and hearing my parents telling on each other, I was surprised that after all the efforts of making my parents proud of me, instead of feeling sad or angry, I actually felt a big relief. But one thing I regret not doing was communicating and preparing my mom for this. Fighting with my own postpartum blues, I was exhausted already and didn't have the energy for more dramas even if I wanted to. So as my dad wished, I never told my mom about our conversation.

Soon after they went back to Shanghai, the divorce was announced. It was an explosion to my mom, a shame, and a scar that could never heal.

I felt that was the darkest time of my life. My parents were divorced; I was raising my first child; working day and night to get research funding and publication during my postdoctoral fellowship training; then pregnant with a second child; and worst of all, I had to deal with my mom after the divorce. What I didn't know was the worst was yet to come.

Dad, Wait for Me, I Am Almost Done with My Grant

In 2007, I got a phone call from my cousin in Australia, who literally shouted at me over the phone questioning when was the last time I called my dad. He told me that my dad was diagnosed with late stage stomach cancer and was in the hospital for surgery. He said you'd better pack to go or you won't see your dad again. That was the last thing I could ever expect. I put down everything and brought along my son and my two-year-old daughter. I bought a whole suitcase of a special healing medicine soup developed by a Japanese doctor who used this to cure thousands of cancer patients. The doctors only gave my dad three months to live. I had to save him by giving him a crash course on wellness and the meaning of life before he left. If he took to the information, maybe he could even be saved. I was certainly very naïve. None of this happened.

I met my dad, his wife, and all his side of the family. Everyone agreed that it was for the best not to tell my dad the truth that he had cancer. With his condition and personality, he could not emotionally handle this news. He just had the best three years in his life after the new marriage. So we decided to tell him that he just had the most severe gastric ulcer and the doctor had to remove most of his stomach away to save him. From then on, he had to rely on feeding tube to get all the medicine and he could only eat certain foods. By the time my dad got out of the hospital, he was happy that it was just an ulcer and he was super happy to see his grandson and granddaughter. What he didn't know was that his tumor grew around a major blood vessel in his stomach and the doctor could not remove it lest he would bleed to death on the surgery table. The doctor removed all what he could remove and embedded some chemo drug in the tumor that remained there. At his age, the doctor wouldn't even recommend further chemo or surgery. Basically, they just sent him home to prepare for death within two to three months. Nevertheless, I was happy to see my dad and see he was happy. I did get a chance to talk to him about all these new discoveries of quantum physics and show him the many thousand-year-old spiritual teachings which may someday turn out to be true and may even be proven by future science. He was intrigued, but it was a little too much for him. At the end, he told me that it was interesting, but I should focus on my scientific research and don't spend too much energy on those things. It could be my hobby to explore and entertain, but don't be too serious about it.

I spent a month with my dad. I didn't know this was the last time I would see him. Before I left, we had a conversation about my mom. My dad said he was sorry that he left behind a mess with me dealing with my mom. He wanted me to take care of my mom but not to feel obligated to agree with her on everything. If anything, don't feel bad to put your own health and your own family first. That turned out to be his last words.

Before I left, I gave my dad a wristband with the word Buddha carved on it. I was not a Buddhist. But many Buddhism teachings and wisdom resonate with me. Besides, in Chinese culture and for my parents' generation, Buddhism is more likely to be accepted than the western new age concepts. My dad accepted. I knew he didn't believe it and was doing that just to acknowledge my goodwill to him.

After I came back, I again dived into my lab work as a junior faculty. Becoming an instructor of medicine meant I needed to get my own research funding to support all my salary and research. That was pretty brutal. But that was how our medical school became so competitive in research. I worked day and night to accumulate preliminary data for a grant application while taking care of my two and five-year-olds. If I could save time from not breathing, going to bathroom, or eating, I would. I did feel I was holding my breath a lot and would not go to the bathroom or go to lunch until I really had to.

However, grant proposals were not easy to become approved as I was just a one-woman lab and you would compete directly with the top scientists and famous professors who had thirty people working in the lab. I was lucky enough to get by with a few awards and publications to be promoted as an assistant professor. But now you not only had to do research, you were also expected to teach, mentor students, and participate in other administrative duties.

I fell in love with teaching and mentoring students. However, I still needed to secure more and more research funding for my lab. I had more ideas and innovations than could be funded.

Each grant I got could only support half or less of what I wanted to do. I had to keep writing more and more grant proposals hoping to get the rest of the research covered. It felt like one could never got out of debt as you promise to deliver project A, and needed the money from project B to finish A, and needed project C to fund project B, and so on. I felt that if I failed to get my research funded, I would lose my job and I didn't know about anything other than doing research and teaching. It was like being in a pressure cooker and had no room for breathing and hope.

Six months after I visited my dad, I was in the middle of an R01 grant proposal submission. R01 grant is considered the standard proof of junior faculty's independent status. Your academic career development depends on that. A week before my grant submission, my dad's wife called to let me know my dad was not doing well. I talked to dad on the phone. He was very weak and I could barely hear him. The last word from him was telling me not to hurry to come visit, and to finish my grant writing first. I quickly finished my proposal and submitted it before I got on the airplane. While I was connecting at Chicago, my sister-in-law texted me that my dad was gone...it was the day after his birthday. His wife later told me, my dad passed away without pain and struggle. Before he left, he had no strength to talk. But he managed to move one of his fingers to point at something. She looked at the direction he was pointing to. It was the Buddha wristband I left him. She helped him to put it on. There was a smile and then tears streamed down his cheeks before he passed in peace.

A few years later, I was attending a conference in a beautiful castle in New York. It was a 100-year-old building. My dad appeared in my dream that night. I never dreamed of any deceased ancestor before. In my dream, my dad was smiling at me. But didn't talk to me. His image was not complete. His face and the top of the body were clear. But his lower body was out of focus. I had no idea what that meant. But I was surprised and happy to see him in my dream. He looked content but not complete. What in his life was not complete? What was he trying to tell me?

After my dad passed away, I went back to Shanghai to pickup his belongings when his poor widow moved. She was diagnosed with cancer afterward as well. My dad didn't finish the whole suitcase of the herb medicine I brought him. He didn't believe in it, nor was he motivated enough to finish it all. He only tried a few while I was there. But his wife was more open and when she was diagnosed with cancer, she tried them and fully recovered. Not sure if this medicine was actually meant for her or if it was what cured her cancer. But I was glad, and I believed that my dad would be happy about that too.

When I was there I got a surprise gift. Before my dad passed away, he told his friend, who was a famous Chinese calligrapher, to write a famous ancient poem where my name was from. It was for my fortieth birthday, a year after my dad passed away. Not to hurt my mom's feelings, I could only hang that beautiful calligraphy in my office. My mom never knew that dad had left that for me.

On the day of my fortieth birthday, my mom bought me a Chinese painting of cherry blossoms in the snow, which was about my name as well. The scenery matches the poem about my name from my dad. I wish I could hang them together some day.

My parents love me and brought me to this world and prepared me with their gift as beloved teachers. They are proud of me. But I was suffering. Suffering from their relationship.

Why did they have to constantly fight over almost everything? Suffering from my own profession. I love teaching and mentoring. But why did I have to struggle with funding and money. Why can't I just teach and mentor without worrying about money? Why do I have to work day and night with no time left to be with my children? I was always in a rush even when I was with them. I rarely had time to listen to them. Nor did I have time to mend my relationship with my mom. All of these also affected my own marriage. I began to fight with my husband like my mom and dad. Things just got worse when he ventured to have his own startup, putting the burden of financial security on my shoulders. Both my mental and physical health started to suffer during this low period of my life.

When we moved to a new town, the kids had to acclimate to their new schools while I was suffering with everything else in my life. My stress affected my son the most and he was bullied on the school bus being the new kid. This caused him to be depressed for a few years. I wasn't there to support, listen, understand, and comfort him. I was so busy with my research and my own emotional struggle to be present for him.

In those years, waves of self-help books hit me just when I needed and kept me floating and inspired me to move on. I literally became a bookworm tirelessly consuming each of these delicious books, from Dr. Michael Newton's *Journey of Souls* and *Destiny of souls*, Dr. Brian Weiss's *Only Love is Real* and *Many Masters Many Messages*, Dr. Brian Greene's *The Elegant Universe* to almost every Abraham Hicks' *Law of Attraction* book and many more other books. A couple of books that totally changed my view of biomedical research that are worth mentioning here are, Dr. Andrew Weil's *Spontaneous Healing*, Dr. Bruce Lipton's *The Biology of Belief*, Dr. Joe Dispenza's

You Are the Placebo, Dr. Colin Campbell's *The China Study*, and Joe Vitale's *Zero Limits*. The more I read, the more I longed for a different life – a life with more love and freedom, a job that allowed for my creativity and teaching but with less stress, and a career that could truly bring sustainable wellness rather than one that's about chasing money for a quick fix. I didn't know my life was about to change...

Chapter 2

Ending My Double Life

They Were Only in Their 50s

On June 17, 2015, my mentor Dr. David Seldin was at home spending his last week with his family. I felt very helpless as I didn't know what to do to save his life. He was the kindest and smartest man I've ever known in my career. He was the chair of my thesis committee meeting, who made every committee meeting so inviting and understanding. I always felt comfortable knowing that I was going to get intelligent advice from him rather than criticism. My thesis mentor, Dr. Thomas Rothstein, another fatherly mentor to me, always encouraged me to seek advice from David. When Tom left BU, he kind of handed me off to David for care. And since then, David became the advocate for my career development. He supported me like no other boss you would ever imagine. As the chief of Hematology Oncology Section of the department, he had to deal with so many things, and yet he would still make phone calls to clinical staff to get me clinical samples I wanted. During a research meeting for allocating lab space to faculty, I requested very small space as a junior faculty. I remember saying, "I don't have grant money to hire lab staffs, why would I need that much space." He firmly corrected me, "You will be successful and you will need an extra bay lab space." In the years after that, I continued to get a minimum amount of research funding, which was one of the biggest struggles to me. Not because my research was bad. As a matter of fact, my research projects were always the most interesting and innovative. It was the lack of believing in myself and the money block I had in me that hindered the flow of money. But I always remember what he said about my lab space, "When there is a will, there is a way." Last summer, I mentored six high school interns and I asked for an extra bay temporarily. Our new chief immediately agreed to let me borrow an extra bay of research space. Lab space was usually assigned to faculty depending on their research funding. After that internship, I returned the space to the department. Then, miraculously, for some reason, that space was given back to my lab permanently. At that moment, I looked at David's picture on the glass door of our lab, I said in my mind, "Is that you, David? Are you there looking over us? Thank you!"

During the last week of his life battling with cancer, David went through many emotional roller coasters. At some point, when another mentor of mine, Dr. Adam Lerner visited him, he was expressing his frustration and left his biggest life question, "Why?" Why did this happen to him? He was kind and smart, and had been treated by the world's top oncologists at Harvard Medical School. Why did he have to die from cancer at fifty-eight years old leaving behind his beloved wife and two daughters? Why?

When Adam told me about this, I was sad and helpless. I went back to the lab and had everyone decorate a piece of paper and put together a sign and hold it for a picture. Then I sent it to him. Later, his wife told us that she held the phone for him to see the picture. He was happy and replied to us "Thank you" with his all his strength. A few days later, he passed away.

A few months before David passed away, another research faculty member in our section, Dr. Anthony Makkinje passed away at age fifty-five. The night before, he worked late and was still able to buy his wife a birthday gift before the store closed. The next morning, he never woke up. Tony had been living with diabetes. He wanted to leave his stressful research job and retire to the countryside of England. His life was cut too short.

When David was diagnosed with cancer, he was full of confidence that this problem would be solved as he had helped many of his patients deal with cancer. He was treated by his colleagues, all of whom were famous oncologists at Harvard Medical School. For three years, he didn't even let anyone know he had cancer, during which time he continued to work as hard as usual, shouldering every problem and issue at the department. When he announced he had cancer and needed to step down from his usual workload, we were all very shocked. During his last few months, not knowing how much time he had left, I suggested he write a book about his life journey as an oncology physician as well as a patient. He thought that was a great idea but he didn't know if he had time to do that. A few months later, he passed away. If he chose to slow down his medical treatment and to write the book of his life, would things have changed? Would he have figured out the biggest why of his life? I don't know. If he chose to write the book, what would he be writing then? If from heaven he wanted to give advice to all those who asks the question, "Should I leave my medical career or not?" What would be his advice?

Taking care of yourself is important no matter what career you choose. Caring for yourself is the biggest gift to the people you love and the people you serve. David knew all the healthy lifestyles and he was a vegetarian. David, Jennifer and I, were eating some junk foods from time to time, getting energy boosts from caffeine, even up to his last few months. One day when I walked in the conference room where we usually had lunch, knowing I was the "healthy guru" on the floor, that was even before I became a health coach, he said "Oho" and then tried to hide the cola can from me. We had good laughs. The biggest joke among students about Dr. Seldin was about how smart he was... so smart that during many of our immunology seminars, he would be too tired to stay awake. He would literally fall asleep in front of the whole room of students and faculty. But he always woke up before the end of the seminar just in time for the Q & A session. And guess what? He would always ask the perfect question to the speaker. That's how hard he worked and how smart he was. But if he could have a way to get more sleep and get more energy without relying on caffeine, would things be different? Probably not entirely. But more sleep and more energy were required for all the faculty on campus.

After Tony and David passed away, the whole Hematology and Oncology Section went into depression. A lot of questions were asked and thought after. But no answers and solutions.

Could This Be My True Calling?

I never expected that the same month when David passed away would be the time I started my journey of becoming a wellness coach. It was one morning, a random Google popup banner ad showed up on my computer screen. It said "Holistic MBA." It caught my curiosity as I had been reading so many self-help, new age books by then to figure out all my life problems and to quench my thirst for the truth. The word "holistic" became my favorite word. But it was never associated with MBA, which to my mind at that time, I associated with money and profit, not holistic. I surrendered to my curiosity and clicked on the Google ad. Little did I know, that click changed my life forever.

For the next six months I enrolled in the Become a Health Coach (BHC) program at the Health Coach Institute, which opened my eyes to the coaching world. It's like entering another world. A true paradigm shift, it felt like as if I lived the past forty-six years just for this moment. I was uplifted and enlightened with every lesson. Literally everything resonated with me. The health coach training is beyond just simple diet or lifestyle change. After six months, I was certified as a health coach and yet I knew what I just learned could not fully quench my thirst for more truth and depth of coaching. I found myself immediately enrolled in the next graduate intensive training in 2016 and then mastery transformational coaching method (TCM) training in 2017 with the wonderful mentors, Stacy Morgenstern and Carey Peters who founded HCI. Carey Peters evolved from her wreckage life of binge eating and body dysmorphia to become a co-founder of a leading coach training company that was earning $30 million in gross revenue by the time I was certified by HCI. Stacy Morgenstern is the oracle coach for which only one word can describe her coaching, "magic." I was among the thousands of coaches who were magnetized by these two women.

Let me tell you the story just to give you an idea of the power of these two women. In 2016, Nicole V. Cramer, a consulting chief of staff and personal brand strategist, food entrepreneur, and speaker, interviewed Carey Peters and wrote a report about HCI on Forbes. She never knew Carey before the interview. After the report, Nicole enrolled the BHC program herself. Nicole certainly had experience and knowledge and was very successful already. It is not the knowledge this health coaching training is about. Certainly, if you have never been in the healthcare field, you will learn a great deal of new knowledge, especially in the first six months of the BHC program. But that is just 20% of what healthy coaching is about. If you are organized and love online research, you probably can be self-taught just by searching online. However, 80% of the coaching is not about knowledge. Most coaches won't really grasp the essence of coaching until they enter the graduate intense and mastery training levels. From that point on, you are teaching less and less, and magically guiding your client more and more. Teaching is for someone you regard as lacking certain knowledge or skills and you will gladly give your knowledge to or help solve problems that person cannot solve. Guiding is different. You no longer see people as being lacking or broken and needing to be fixed. You see them as 100% capable and as intelligent as Einstein and as wise as Buddha. You can see and hold the vision of their best version of themselves and the vision of their dream life for them until they can see and create it by themselves. That's the magic transformation of TCM coaching.

As Dr. Stephen R. Covey once said, "If you want small changes in your life, work on your attitude. But if you want big and primary changes, work on your paradigm."

Here are the thirteen paradigms that transformed me and are what my coaching is based on. These are the paradigms that totally changed the lives of those I coached.

1. Big issues require little changes
2. Beliefs create our experiences
3. A master TCM coach works with beliefs and identity
4. Every time we are confronted with moving forward, we are also confronted with allowing someone else to stay where they are
5. We live in a mirroring universe and [there is] nothing we experience that we do not create

6. All parents love their children. The only variable is whether this love will be demonstrated congruently and beautifully or become twisted and so severely deformed that it is not recognizable as love.
7. There are only two experiences that are intolerable for children. To not know the rules of how life works and to not belong.
8. In the family system, children are eager to be the source of the problem so that they can hope to be the source of the solution
9. The experiences we learn to survive become the conditions upon which our continued survival depends
10. The source of suffering is the way we suffer for other people in an unworkable effort to say, "I love you"
11. Today's limiting belief was yesterday's solution
12. As coaches we cannot expect to take our clients farther than we ourselves are willing to go
13. Each of us has a legacy of ecology making being okay not okay

Understanding these paradigms totally changed my perspective of parenting and relationships. I not only started to understand my parents, their love for me, and why their marriage didn't work out, but practicing these paradigms also helped me to transform my way of parenting and my relationship with my husband and his family and everyone I encountered in my life.

The way I changed my clients' lives surprised me. Unlike a physician, if you treat a patient with medicine and medical procedure, you can pretty much predict how things will turn out. But coaching people at mastery level, you will be surprised and amazed by the outcomes.

This Is Beyond My Scientific Training

Cathy (not her real name) went into my office with pain almost everywhere in her body – headache, neck pain, muscle soreness, you name it. She badly wanted a promotion at work. She was upset that her supervisor was not taking her contributions seriously. Three weeks into TCM coaching, she told me she was feeling much better than the past three years going to her psychiatrist office for her anxiety, which she never mentioned to me during our previous coaching sessions. She told her psychiatrist that she was seeing me and getting health coaching. Her psychiatrist was not happy. She had all the reason to feel that way. Because soon after, Cathy no longer had a need for her psychiatrist. By the time we finished, twelve weeks of coaching, all her body pain and her anxiety were gone. She was happy and I was happy. I thought that was it. Then a few days later, she emailed me, "Got my labs back from last week and my numbers have never been this good... I owe you and your wellness coaching a BIG THANK YOU!!!" When I looked at her numbers, it was clinically impossible to achieve those results with regular medicine in just ninety days. Her numbers were bad for years. The surprises didn't stop there. She started to visit her father who had been in a bad relationship with her for years. They started to talk. And she got her promotion at work. The following Thanksgiving, Cathy emailed me, "I am grateful to you for helping me change my outlook on life. My life is immeasurably better after working with you!"

The magic of the TCM coaching is not just how many things in life can be changed. Sometimes I was just blown away by how fast it can change. I met a fellow coach during a retreat event. We laser coached each other, an intense, fast coaching method for clients who are in a super coachable state. She had autoimmune diseases and had a difficult time conceiving. She had been seeing doctors and trying different diets. During the coaching, something led us to a totally unexpected area of her life. She revealed something buried deep inside her so deep that she almost forgot herself and something that she had never told another soul. A year later, she gave birth to her first child followed by another a year later. Her previously endangered marriage turned into the best happily-ever-after fairy tale.

I started by coaching people with health issues. But soon I found myself, helping people way beyond their health issues.

Leila (not her real name) could not afford to pay her already subsidized low rent when I started working with her. She was extremely insecure and had all her windows closed and shades down even in the daytime. Her walls were all painted a dark color. She would put all the locks on the doors and turn on the security alarm system. Even though she was in a nice and safe neighborhood, her insecurity and anxiety constantly limited all aspects of her life. After twelve weeks of deep coaching, we removed the root of her insecurity and she was totally at a different place in her life. She paid all her debt and she landed her dream job at a hospital and doubled her income! When she invited me over, I was shocked. She showed me all her rooms, which were now painted light color and her furniture was changed into all light colors. And she looked fabulous, like a fashion model. She literally was a different person. A year later, she texted me, "Things are going so well that I feel every day is a blessing. Things are so much better than before. Totally different... You helped change my life in more ways than you think... If there were more people like you in this world, life would be so different for a lot of people!"

These are just a few of the many clients' stories that surprised me. They confirmed what I had always been suspecting, that I was born to do this and I am gifted to be a life coach. Leila's comment reminded me of my mission to devote the rest of my life to help people live a joyful, purposeful, and fulfilling life. This became my mission statement, "When the amount of people living a satisfactorily fulfilling life reaches a critical mass, the earthly human experience will leap into a currently unimaginable bliss." And I named my coaching business, HOE Holistic Wellness, where HOE was HOPE with the "P" removed. "P" stands for all the things that Prevent us from living that satisfactory and fulfilling life. I want people to "Stop Hoping, Start Be-living" so that they can literally experience Heaven On Earth (HOE).

Wait, How Am I Going to Make a Living with This?

I was so determined and excited that I found my dream job and purpose. It was time to transition from disease-care to true health-care! I registered my business, set up my website and really wanted to move forward to my new life. However, there was one thing I didn't mention. One thing that became the last and biggest hurdle for me to quit my medical school professor job in order to have my full-time dream job as a wellness and life coach. That was, I didn't know how to get paid for coaching. Yes, we were taught many ways how to set pricing, how to build up a coaching program, how to advertise, and get our message out. But I was hesitant to quit my job before I could see that I could make money with coaching. Because I still had a full-time job at the medical school, the time I could use for building business and coaching was so limited. And I fell into the conundrum that in order to build a coaching business,

I needed to quit my job so I would have more time to do that. On the other hand, in order to quit my job, I needed the income to replace my salary. At that point, I already invested more than $30k for the training and my family started to panic about my expensive "hobby" of coaching.

To make matters worse, I just kept on giving free coaching. Something was wrong. Every time I opened my mouth asking for the payment, the words just came out to be "I will coach you for free. Don't worry about the money." Deep down in my mind, I was here to save people's lives, like Jesus, Mother Teresa, Mahatma Gandhi, and it was supposed to be not-for-profit. I could take donations but never a payment nor profit. How could I ask people for money when they were sick and poor when I coached them? I felt I would be exploiting them if I did. They could not afford it anyway.

Something had to change or I would be stuck at my old job doing research, bored to death from applying for grant after grant, seeking approval by doing what was considered the norm. Every research proposal had to declare that it would end up a novel drug or treatment or you wouldn't be funded. With all the people's lives I changed with my coaching, I just could not see myself continuing to burn myself out by studying diseases and creating more pills for people to swallow. How can we as medical professions take care of general public while being so sick ourselves? But if I quit, I would starve to death on my undervalued dream job and could not help anyone. Knowing my dream job is out there and yet not being able to make the final decision felt even worse than not knowing the option at all. Every day I was living a double life and I was tormented. The whole idea of leaving my biomedical career was to be able to have time for self-care and to serve others better. But this double life made me even busier and more stressed. It felt like standing on burning coals with my feet shackled, watching others crossing over to the dreamland. I fell into another rabbit hole for another year until I met my next two mentors, Bill Baren and Dr. Angela Lauria.

Chapter 3

Ask and You Shall Receive

The Big Shift

As I was struggling with shifting my money mindset, my mastermind coach told me there was going to be a three-day Money Impact Intensive small group workshop led by Bill Baren, the oracle business coach. I watched Bill coaching on stage at a coaching retreat. No words are better than "oracle business coach" to describe him. As an introvert, I had never been on the hot seat in front of hundreds of fellow students during HCI training. I was longing for small group training where I would have no place to hide. This sounded like the perfect workshop and perfect timing to end my struggle. And it turned out to be totally transformational!

Like what Stacy Morgenstern often reminds us during coaching training, "Nothing happens to you. Everything is happening for you." This event was the Universe's answer to my struggle.

Bill's workshops are often spontaneous and have dramatic turns. During this workshop, I witnessed one magic moment after another. The most amazing of all was the muscle testing, which was totally unplanned. The first time I learned about muscle testing was reading from Dr. Bruce H. Lipton's book, *The Biology of Belief.* As a spiritual scientist, I resonate so much with Dr. Lipton's path and discovery. Later, I learned more about muscle testing from Dr. David Hawkins' book *Power vs. Force* but I had never witnessed in person how powerful this was until Bill's workshop.

At the beginning of the workshop, Bill asked how many of us believed we would become a six-figure coach. Every one raised their hands. Talking about positive thinking and intention! We thought we were good coaches. Then Bill said, just because you said you believe in something doesn't mean you truly believe it. He asked if we would like to be muscle tested. That reminded me the book title, "Your body doesn't lie" by Dr. John Diamond, who was the pioneer of applying muscle testing in medical practice. Now everyone in the classroom was excited and curious to see who was a six-figure coach.

As well-trained coaches, we all know we are the creators of our own life. We have to believe before we see it. When you truly believe in something, 99% of your creation is done. That literally means you have a 99% chance to become a six-figure coach. It would just be a matter of time for the universe to coordinate the manifestation. There were thirty of us in the classroom. Bill went around and muscle tested every single one of us. Guess how many of us were 99% sure of becoming a six-figure coach? Two!!! And I was not one of them. We were all amazed, and a little disappointed, but eager to move on with the training as Bill foresaw that by the end of the training, a majority of us would feel like we could be six-figure coaches. I was very impressed. But what happened next was beyond my imagination.

During the next three days, Bill would stop at a seemingly random moment, and call on one of us to get onto the stage to do the muscle testing when he sensed that coach was ready, and 100% of the time he was correct. A few of us were so eager and thought we were ready to be tested. But Bill said, "Sorry, not yet." When he saw the disappointed faces, he would entertain us by inviting the disappointed coach on the stage. "We can test it if you don't believe me," he would say. The result? You guessed it. They were not ready. We had so much fun when one of the coaches was tested, ready to be a six-figure coach, but then she was so confident that she believed she was even ready for a seven-figure coach. Bill said, "I don't think so. But we can try." Again, he was right.

During a break, to avoid the crowd in the bathroom, I went back to my hotel room. The spring rain had just stopped and the mountain view from my balcony was like a fresh oil painting. It was such a tranquil and beautiful moment and suddenly a thought appeared in my mind out of nowhere. "Enjoy the moment." I remember the night before, at the fireside chat, Bill coached me to live in the moment. Not that I hadn't heard of this before, but somehow, it was so powerful and personal. I thought that was the moment I was living in. But the thought continued, "Enjoy this beautiful moment while you can." It was definitely not the logical thinking of my mind. But the next moment, I had goose bumps all over when the thought continued further, "You will be so busy coaching like Bill. You won't even have time to stop and enjoy what you are doing now." My tears started to pour and I was showered with unspoken love when the thought continued, "Silly child, why do you have to worry about finding clients and getting paid for coaching? You are given this time to get ready. Enjoy while you can..." And then the thoughts stopped there for me to go back to the classroom. At that time, I was crying and trembling unstoppably. Not knowing what was going on, one of my classmates hugged me and held me tightly while I was trembling. That's the beauty of the coach tribe. There is always love and support you can count on.

At that moment, I knew I was ready to be a six-figure coach. It was more about the responsibility and the soul contract I felt than a business strategy. But I was surprised I didn't get called upon the stage to be tested for the rest of the day. My logical mind started its usual business. "Was that just a coincident or hallucination?" it doubted and cautioned. But the excitement and transformational coaching moment after moment quieted my logical mind.

It was at the end of the training, we were in a circle ready to wrap up, when Bill walked over to me, "You have something to share?" he smiled. It was a smile that could see through you, leaving your energy and your thoughts no place to hide nor pretend. He knew I was waiting. He then handed me the microphone and made a funny pulling gesture as if he was pulling an invisible line and getting me to the center of the circle. I stood there, totally open, confident, clear, and feeling so much love that my love had to spill out to every one in the classroom. I shared my experience, delivered the message. It was my alter ego, the dragon, who delivered the powerful and fun speech. Then, the moment arrived. Bill walked to me and raised my arm for the muscle testing. The whole classroom was filled with joyful laughs. I passed the test.

To Bill, the ultimate business strategy is to serve with compassion and responsibility. To have a coaching business is to have a loving relationship with your clients, including tough love sometimes, which was one of the reasons I had trouble asking for payment. But the bottom line is, everything has to come from that loving place, which sometimes takes a lifetime practice to master.

After coming back from Bill's workshop, I finally came out from hiding in the closet of doubting, questioning, and being cautious. I had so much to give and I felt the responsibility of being a messenger and the burden of delivering all the messages that I had been holding for so long. From HCI and Bill's workshop, for the first time in my whole life, I did a Facebook Live. Not just one, but a ten-week live series. For me, this was a big deal. As a perfectionist, I always wanted to wait until everything was perfect. I had to look perfect and my speech had to be prepared and polished; to do a Facebook Live would be suicidal. I could teach in-person in the medical school classroom, knowing my material like the back of my hand and knowing my students were often too busy taking notes to notice or would not care if anything was wrong with my outfit. But Facebook Live is a totally different experience. With Facebook Live there may be no one listening or someone may randomly pop-up, and you would have no idea who and when you are seen and heard, and you have no idea what kinds of comments there might be. Facing the unknown is one of the driving factors of fear.

But I was a different person now. My alter ego had his voice and he showed up now. I had become empowered and balanced.

The name of the series was called "The Pajama Talk" where I delivered messages I received the week of the Facebook Live in my pajamas. The whole idea, not sure it was coming from my logic mind or a result of co-creation with my higher self, was to let people know they could live a fun and joyful life without prolonged struggle. I do collect thoughts in the morning to write down on my notebook. But I never knew I was supposed to talk about any of the written ones or the ones that pop out the day before the live event. And I was in total peace that for the first time in my life as I was delivering talks without knowing the topic ahead of time. When I am on Facebook Live, I have a few lines of notes and a few inspired figures for illustration. That was totally not me as a medical school professor. I am a different person now. That was the transformation of life coaching.

The Pajama Group currently consists of more than sixty members. I didn't want to do a public live event as I only wanted to deliver messages to those who are open-minded, nonjudgmental, and willing to transform themselves. These days, even a click of a link to join the group is a huge effort and a gesture of willingness. The messages I downloaded were well-received in the group. But how can I deliver to more people who are seeking and willing to open themselves for a life upgrade?

When a question is asked, the Universe has to deliver the answer.

This is how I met my next mentor and the birth of this book.

What Are You Waiting For?

I heard about Dr. Angela Lauria through the Internet and YouTube quite a while ago. I was fascinated with The Author Castle and her business model. Her mission to help life coaches find their voices and build their platforms through books really impressed me. I dreamed to be like a princess author in the castle. But the elegance of the castle also prevented me from joining, as I would imagine the price tag must also be quite "fascinating."

Shortly after I went back to Boston following Bill's workshop, I received one of the many webinar announcement emails from The Author Incubator. Maybe I was still riding the momentum of the workshop, this time, something was calling me. I signed up for the webinar, but for some reason I was late, only catching the last few minutes. But this is the magic, when the time is right; when the client is ready; no words are needed. I was totally sold. I gladly applied for The Author Incubator and waited for the exciting news that I was accepted into the program. I was told Dr. Angela only accepts 25 applicants out of more than 2,000 every month and she only works with those who have soul contracts with her, who has a message, mission, and was born to make a difference. Feeling the connection, I am very much expected to write a book to reach the people who I have a soul contract within this life. I remember early in my health coach training at HCI, we were practicing a mental rehearsal and we did a time travel exercise, and I saw in my mind's eye a long line of people waiting for me. I could not see the end of the line. And the thoughts I received during Bill's training and many other incidences were all calling out to me, "What are you waiting for?" And here I am writing this book with my coach, Dr. Angela and her team!

Without all my mentors and coaches, I would not be able to be here writing this book. But there is one more person I have to mention, without whom I would not be writing on this particular topic. That's Matthew Reynolds.

Quitting Medical School? Are You out of Your Mind?

You never would expect how the universe answers you until looking back when all the dots can be clearly connected.

In October 2018, I was invited to attend an education event for a non-profit organization that brought education and connection between clinical trials of new medical treatments or devices and the patients who would like to participate in clinical trials. This event sounded very medical and scientifically-oriented and seemed to be a great opportunity for medical researchers and clinical scientists to connect with pharmaceutical companies and potential clinical trial patients. It would be fitting for me if I wanted to promote the new discovery of my Immuno-Oncology research and new potential cancer treatment. But at that point, as I was so determined to quit my research job, I was not sure if I would be of any help. When I asked the host, I was told I was welcome to promote my wellness coaching as a sponsor. Despite not feeling that this was a best-fit event, I went there anyway. During the event, I brought out some fun little games to introduce wellness coaching and the attendees could win some free coaching sessions. I didn't expect that our little table became an instant hotspot of the event. But what surprised me the most was an email I received two months later.

It was from Matt Reynolds, a first-year medical school student from Tufts University School of Medicine. In his email, he said, "...one of my professors mentioned "winning" a coaching session with you recently. It came up when I was talking to her about whether I wanted to continue to pursue medicine or rather, if how I want to help people is more in the area of coaching. As a result, I'd love to have a brief chat with you about getting into coaching!"

I thought I was the oddball in my medical school community. I could understand that many burnt-out nurses or therapists found coaching a better way to help their patients. But a first-year medical school student who wants to quit medical school was not something I expected. I was so intrigued. I ended up talking to Matt over the phone for almost two hours helping him to decide if health coaching was the right choice for him and if he should quit medical school. From our conversation, I was so impressed by his discovery of his passion and insight into the current medical and healthcare system. Considering the fact that Matt graduated from Vanderbilt, the Harvard of the South, got his MPH, and was a first-year medical school student, with other physicians in his family, he could easily have had a bright future with a stable income and social status. But he was determined. A few months later, when we got reconnected, Matt already enrolled into a life coach-training program and was on his way to become a health coach. By mentoring medical school students for almost two decades and loving my students as if they were my own children, I habitually wanted so much to help young brilliant students like Matt. Knowing that making decisions is not easy, and that many do so out of social pressures, and understanding that the path after the decision is made is far from rosy, I find my purpose in supporting all those who are on this path with this book and my coaching!

You can find my interview with Matt and many others who have already quit their medical career or in the process of transitioning out of it, with this link to the Pajama Group:

https://www.facebook.com/groups/393323931238303/

The stories of the people I interviewed motivated me to write this book with all my heart and to incorporate all that I have learned during my path of transition.

You Are Not Alone and Here Are the Shocking Stats

If you are reading this book now, you are probably thinking of quitting your medical career or biomedical research career and feeling it very challenging to make the decision.

You are not alone!

Statistically, and ironically, medical professionals are one of the least healthy professional groups as compared to the general public who the medical professionals were supposed to serve and make them healthier. It was reported in the news that many medical professionals, even established physicians, are thinking of a career change. Not only that, in recent years medical scientists with PhD degrees are having the highest dropout rate in history. According to a research paper published on December 10, 2018 in the journal of the Proceedings of the National Academy of Sciences (PNAS), which tracked more than 100,000 scientific careers, 50% of the people pursuing careers as scientists at higher education institutions drop out of the field after five years, which is the highest it's been in fifty years.

In a landmark 2014 Proceedings of the National Academy of Science (PNAS) article "Rescuing US biomedical research from its systemic flaws" and its 2015 follow up article "Addressing systemic problems in the biomedical research enterprise," Dr. Bruce Alberts, from UCLA, Dr. Marc W. Kirschner from Harvard Medical School, Dr. Shirley Tilghman from Princeton University, and Dr. Harold Varmus from National Cancer Institute (NCI) pointed out that the US biomedical research ecosystem has become "an unsustainable hypercompetitive system" that is "a recipe for long-term decline." The systemic flaws are currently enormously underestimated at all levels:

- At young student level: The rapid biotech advances in the previous decades still give the incoming students the illusion that there are plenty of academic jobs waiting for them after graduation, without realizing only 20% will have their academic scientist dream come true. 80% of the students will not be adequately prepared for alternative jobs and will be underemployed by continuous postdoctoral training and soft positions in the universities without a formal job
- At institution level: Profiting from indirect cost from research grants and cheap labor and training-centered research systems become more and more problematic for job-related stress and toxic hypercompetitive working environments
- At government level: With increasing federal funding becoming more and more of an unrealistic dream, competition between established and young incoming scientists is driving science more and more towards profitable translational science and the imagination and creativity of young scientists are greatly suppressed

Thirty prominent senior scientists in the biomedical field gathered to validate the situation and tried to brainstorm solutions as a follow-up action of the 2014 publication. But unfortunately, they concluded that not much could be done at the government and the institution level, and realized that only a movement from the grassroots level might reshape the system.

The article concluded that "The stakes are enormous: the current environment is beginning to erode the remarkable opportunities created over past decades to advance our understanding of biological systems and to improve the health of the public."

On the other side of the US medical system, physicians are increasingly suffering another series of systemic flaws. After decades of training from medical school, residency, to fellow, physicians and nurses were trained to work long hours and to be heroic. However, this model is becoming more and more unsustainable as well. According to a study published in Mayo Clinic Proceedings, 54.4% (n=3,680) of the 6,880 physicians who completed surveys reported at least one symptom of burnout.

According to the "National Physician Burnout, Depression & Suicide Report 2019," burnout has been defined as long-term unresolvable job stress that leads to exhaustion, feeling overwhelmed, and lacking a sense of personal accomplishment. According to this report, 44% of physicians experience burnout, 11% are colloquially depressed and 4% are clinically depressed, 14% had thoughts of suicide. The top 10 burnout contributing factors are:

1. Too many bureaucratic tasks
2. Spending too many hours at work
3. Increasing computerization of practice
4. Lack of respect at work place
5. Insufficient compensation
6. Lack of control/autonomy
7. Government regulations
8. Feeling like just a cog in a wheel
9. Emphasis on profits over patients
10. Lack of respect from patients

These not only affect physicians and nurses but also affect their family members and patients.

In 2017, a Facebook group called the "Drop Out Club" reached 37,000 members. These were people who are desperate physicians who find and counsel each other on quitting the field. Later this site became a 52,283-members docjobs.com searching for "innovative careers for doctors, scientists, and healthcare professionals."

While so many highly educated and brilliant physicians and scientists are struggling and desperately searching to find a career that can serve their original purpose while having a work-life balance, I could no longer sit there buried under the messages that were meant to help them transition.

So How Is This Book Going to Help You?

Nowadays we have GPS and we just turn it on, trusting it to guide us to our destination. In the old days, when there was no GPS, before I went on a trip to someplace I didn't know, I would study the big map very hard, trying to remember exactly where I should turn, where I should stop for food and gas. It was literally a big map book, which I remember I got from AAA. It was very heavy and hard to turn. Whenever I got lost, which happened almost every time during a long trip, I would stop the car and get to the back seats to flip through the gigantic map book.

Even these days with GPS, I still feel better when I have a big picture of a general direction and destination on the Google map before I head out using GPS. Having a map in your head is also helpful when the weather turns bad or when you venture into a remote area where there is little or no signal.

The moment you ask if I should leave my current job or not is the moment you are actually planning your life adventure to a new place, regardless if you end up staying at your current job or launching a new career. Even if at the end of reading this book or working with me in person, you decide to stay in your current career path, you will be at a totally new place. That could mean you get a promotion, a new way of working or start a new movement at your current position that will be way more satisfying than where you are now.

Since this is an adventure, what I offer you with this book is a GPS and a map that you can refer to whenever and wherever you need during this important adventure of your life.

Ever since I started my journey of becoming a life coach, there have been moments of excitement and clarity, as well as periods of doubt and disappointment. There were times when the hard challenges hit me, when I wanted to give up and go back to my old job and old way of living. Those are like the times I traveled to remote areas with no GPS signal and not knowing how to connect and get back on track.

Looking back, I wish I had this book, a map with an overview of what I would experience, which way to turn, just like those pins to mark the important pitfalls on your path so you don't fall for them. In this book, I will also give you tools to connect to your inner wisdom when you need it. That is like a GPS you can always trust.

You are not eighteen years old, influenced by parents, or by peer pressure or social expectations. This is your second chance of connecting to your own purpose and calling. This book is to help you make the easy but inspired and empowered choices toward finding the career that is truly meant for you. It may still be medical or it may not be. The key is to find your own calling and be fully prepared for the tests and bumps after the decision is made. So you will have the tools, the GPS, the map to keep you on track and moving forward without regret.

After you make the decision, it is 100% certain there will be plenty of tests down the road where you will ask yourself if you made the right decision or if you should go back to the medical field where a decent paycheck is desirable because you are not sure how you will be paid or if you can find your next client. When you have a big test ahead, what do you do? Study hard and plan ahead of time? Ask help from your teacher? Get a tutor? Practice and more practice? You'll do some or all of these things until you feel so confident and so ready that you can't wait for the test. On the test day, what's a big mountain to others will be such a piece of cake for you. This is what this book is for.

Based on all the training, research, and direct-download from the higher place, I created a 7-step process just for you to help you get ready for your big transition in your life. I call this process UPLEVEL.

U for Unload
P for Purpose
L for Leverage
E for Envision
V for Voice
E for Empower
L for Level

Now, are you ready to learn the 7-step UPLEVEL process I prepared for you?

Part 2

The 7-Step UPLEVEL Process

Chapter 4

Step 1: U for Unload

(Unload the Problem, Sitting Back, and Watch the Movie)

"Nature is not in a hurry, but left nothing undone."
– Lao Zi (Lao Tzu)

How Can I Relax With Such a Big Decision to Make?

Yes, I hear you. I've been there. "Should I quit my medical profession or not?" is more than just one question. It comes with a bonus package of hundreds of questions and a gigantic crossroad to make you feel safer to just not making any decision.

On one side of the road, you are suffering from long hours of work, burnout, and overloaded with endless responsibilities of being a physician, NP, or medical scientists, the tensions of staffing, mentor-mentee training, endless deadlines, shortage of funding and human resources. All-in-all, your own sense of wellbeing wasn't even in the picture.

On the other side of the road, the word "quitting" was never taught in your medical training. With the social stage set so high for medical profession, you almost left with not many alternative choices you can see that might be equally recognized and appreciated at the moment.

"What career path should I take if I quit?"

"Will I still be able to keep my financial and social status while having more time for myself and my family?"

"What will my parents think?"

"What will my husband/wife think?"

"Will I look like a quitter or loser? Will my children still look up to me for inspiration?"

"Am I going to waste all these years of training and financial investment?"

"Who will I be?"

Unload Your Frustration

The first step of the process I want you to take is to unload all of those frustrations from your head and shoulders or anywhere in your body that you feel the most tension. Right now. Take a deep breath, sit back, and watch a movie of your life.

I know this is weird. But bear with me. Continue reading and you will know why and get the "wow" coming at the end of this chapter.

My Son's Piano Performance Stage Fright

When my son was born, the whole family had very high expectations of him. He is the first grandchild of both my and my husband's family. Like many Chinese families, playing the piano becomes the symbol of a good childhood education even if music was never a thing in the family. My son was an adorable and smart baby. Not learning piano was not an option. He started at five years old. By age seven, he already played complicated pieces without the piano sheet. We blindly believed he was going to be the Mozart of our family. Finally, it was time to put something on his resume for his college application. Talking about early bird! The piano school, run by a Russian pianist, arranged the students to participate in an international contest. But to encourage students, basically everyone considered by the teacher as ready was selected to compete for an award. An audition was just a matter of formality. But my son didn't know this. So when the time came for him to play in front of a stranger for the audition, he totally panicked. I never saw him nervous like that. He was sitting there waiting for his turn with his face all squared without a smile. His hands were cold, his legs were shaking, and his head was down looking at the floor. Finally, when it was his turn, he played a few notes and then he thought he made a mistake. He was panicking and suddenly buried his face into his hands and wouldn't play anymore. The audition pianist was very patient and tried to make him comfortable. But he was still very nervous and refused to play anymore. Finally, the head of the piano school came, laughed, and assured him that according to his performance at his class, he was already qualified and got an award. The audition was just a formality to make sure you could play on stage in New York for the award ceremony. My son was still very confused with all these adults and their arrangement of the whole competition thing. But somehow he was able to move on with the audition.

If my son knew no matter how he performed during this audition, his piano performance skills were recognized already, with the award and certificate for him already printed out and waiting for him, then his fear of making a mistake and not getting recognized, or disappointing his mom or the teacher, was totally unnecessary.

As a matter of fact, not many people realize that life is very similar.

Try to wrap your mind around this: If we knew our dream life is already there waiting for us, what's the hurry? What's the frustration then?

I know this may sounds very strange and not scientific. So here's an idea of what the feeling is like.

In 1987, I was nineteen years old, a freshman in college in Shanghai. I was busy studying and had no idea what my life would be in the future. All I knew was to study hard and get good grades so I could land a good job to make my parents proud. All I could see was what was right in front of me. The lectures to take, the books to read, the exams to take. I never thought of anything beyond a year. I never thought of going to US and had no idea that in six years I would leave this country and spend the rest of my life so far away.

Meanwhile, on the other side of the earth, in a small town twenty-two miles outside of Boston, a developer was building a whole new community and one of the houses they were building was my future house. It took twenty-three years for me to move all the way from the other side of the earth to this continent and into that house. This house, which I call home now, already existed in 1987. But it was totally out of my awareness.

Just contemplate that. What if your future job and your future life already out there exist in a gigantic warehouse? What if your job is just to shed light on it and pick it up?

What If Your Future Already Exists?

Now you may argue, yes, your future house existed. But it could be any of the houses. You just happened to choose that one. Yes, that's exactly the other point I wanted to make. Not only your future exists already, you also have choices.

It is a very odd thing to think that whatever we want is already existing in the future whether we are aware of it or not. So we don't have to make effort to build it from scratch. Now this sounds totally absurd and is totally against the virtue I grew up with. I was always taught to work hard to get something or earn something. It is neither fair nor possible to get something without hardworking or effort.

However, ancient wisdom from thousands of years and modern quantum physics of the past century, have been disagreeing with this "hardworking" virtue.

In his words left to the world before he disappeared, ancient Chinese spiritual teacher Lao Zi taught this mysterious "Non-Action" concept. As I quoted at the beginning, "Nature is not in a hurry, but left nothing undone." is one of many of his famous teachings in the book of Tao De Jing, which is one of the most translated books only second to the Bible.

It would make sense if everything we ever wanted were already there, then there is absolutely no reason to worry nor hurry. Just like if we want something these days, we order from Amazon and they will deliver the next day or you can pick up the same day. So what's the worry and hurry? However, these days we want more and more but our senses of certainty and security are less and less. We don't know if we will get it or not. Even if we get it, we don't know if we will get it again or get a better one. Constant doubt and fear are the main drivers for our stressful modern-day lifestyle and that stress is eating us alive.

Yes, it would be nice if everything we ever wanted were already there as if it were in a gigantic warehouse. But the question is, how can everything be there already? If I have to make a decision to quit my job or stay at my job, the outcome will be very different. Do both future outcomes already exist?

Quantum physicists have been trying to solve the same mystery for the past 100 years. If you can recall your high school physics, you may remember the famous double-slit experiment. In the first experiment, Thomas Young tested light and found that light has wave-particle duality. When there is no observer present, light is in the form of a wave and can simultaneously pass both slits. Whereas once an observer was present, light become particle-like and can only pass one slit at a time. Later, Clinton Davisson and Lester Germer showed electrons also behave the same way. But most interesting, hence the mystery, is that an observer can influence the nature of light, or any quantum particle (electron, atom, or even bigger molecules). Before the observation, these particles can simultaneously exist in different locations until an observer appeared. This is when the simultaneous existences of all possibilities collapsed into what resonates with the observer. That possibility becomes the observer's reality and all the other possibilities would seem to the observer as having never existed.

In quantum physics, such manifestation of one of many possibilities (quantum states) into so-called reality is called "Wave Function Collapse." In order for such collapse to happen, the possibilities will have to interact with the "observer" external of the quantum system. If we can understand and practice such quantum collapse, then pulling things out of thin air, like Jesus feeding people with 500 loafs of bread out of thin air or walking on water would be an everyday routine rather than a miracle or a legend.

The reality most of us choose to live in is a linear time space with much less possibilities and flexibilities. Making a decision like, "Should I quit my medical career or not?" would be very frustrating. Because most of us do not realize that all is possible and tangible and we have the absolute freedom to choose the best of what we desire. Because of this inherited "ignorance," we have the illusion that we cannot have it all. If we have something, we must give it up or sacrifice something else. Therefore, we have to choose carefully and if we make one wrong move, we will lose big. This is why making a life decision like this is so hard.

Just like my son, if he knew he would be performing on stage in New York regardless of how he performed during that audition, then ironically he would not have panicked and he would have performed as beautifully as he did during his practices and lessons. If he ever knew, if he could have just enjoyed playing piano and never need to worry if he is good enough or if his mom and dad would be proud of him or not.

So am I suggesting we just relax and sit there waiting for our future to happen? Absolutely not.

You Have Plenty of Choices

The other day I was chaperoning my daughter's school trip to the Canobie Lake Park. It is a popular theme park not far from Boston. I brought my computer with me to work on this manuscript. I picked a perfect picnic table by the lake where I could keep an eye on the kids if they needed me. It was a beautiful day and everyone was grateful and happy. Watching kids running from one ride to another, hearing them screaming down the roller coaster, I just realized that no one was complaining and suffering even when they failed on any challenge. They just laugh about it, keep trying, or just pick a different ride. I never saw any kid having a hard time choosing or moving on from one ride to another, or getting so confused or upset that they couldn't accomplish any ride. I asked myself, wasn't life supposed to be as fun as this? What if life is an adventure theme park experience? What if your soul just wants the excitement, the joy, and the creation? While you are screaming down life's roller coaster, your soul is actually satisfied with the excitement. But why do we feel suffering with all kinds of life experiences? Why we are having so much of a hard time picking our rides? Because we forget why we are here? Because we disconnect from our soul and only use our logical mind to run things. We forget we are in a "theme park" and have plenty of choices. We forget that we have the security system there and we can hardly fail. The sense of lost control is momentary when we lose the sense of gravity. But when we forget that we are actually always safe, it makes us feel the momentary lost of control will last forever in what we call "real life."

Remember, we do have choices. To make a choice is to distinguish what we truly desire and what we do not desire, which we will talk about in the next chapter.

So for now, I want you to really absorb these ideas:

1. Everything you possibly need or want is already there
2. Your job is no longer learning to survive
3. Your job is to choose what you want and thrive
4. The purposes of your life are joy and creation

For the rest of the book, I will guide you to be crystal clear what you really want and practice to resonate your thoughts, feelings, and energy with it so that you can quantum collapse that reality. Human suffering is often rooted in forgetting what we truly desire, and focusing on the unwanted and therefore collapsing the undesired reality without knowing. Our misery is further perpetuated by being stuck in the undesired condition without knowing we actually have choices.

So step one of the decision-making process is to unload your problems and frustrations, sit back and watch a movie of your life. This step serves two purposes.

The first purpose is to unload all the thoughts about the problems and issues that made you nervous and worried if this "leaving the medical career thing" could be a big mistake. Without unloading those heavy thoughts, you will not be able to have a front row clear view of your life movie. Neuroscientists discovered that if you are constantly in a fight or flight mood, your brain will distribute most of the blood to your brain stem to support your survival. But your emotions and logical thinking will be reduced to conserve energy for the muscles etc. for the fight or flight. Unloading your problem will release you from the fight or flight mode and allow you to have a clearer thought process and open you up to the many ideas and opportunities that you would not have had otherwise. If you move on without unloading all your problems, it would be like sitting in the theater blindfolded and wearing earplugs.

The second purpose is to change your perspective from being the character in the movie to an observer. As a character in a movie, you always want to be in a specific moment or a frame of the film. You would not be able to be in the past or future. But as an observer, you don't have to be in the "now" frame and you can rewind the movie to the past as well as forward to the future. Basically you will be open and positioned to all possibilities for you to choose from.

Ultimately, by sitting back as an observer instead of the character, you'll have a front row view so you can create, choose, and quantum collapse the possibility that resonates with you the best. Are you ready for the movie?

I would love to hear what you think so far. To contact me for any questions or if you want me to guide you through this process, email: support@hoeholisticwellness.com

Notes

_____

_____

_____

_____

_____

_____

_____

_____

_____

_____

_____

_____

_____

_____

_____

_____

_____

_____

Chapter 5

Step 2: P for Purpose

(Reclaim Your Purpose)

*"At the center of your being you have the answer;
you know who you are and you know what you want."*
– Lao Tzu

Didn't I Always Know What I Want?

The first part of Step 2 is knowing what you want.

One of my favorite teachers, Abraham-Hicks, often starts her workshops by asking, "Do you know what you want?" Almost everyone says, "Of course, I know what I want." But then she replies, "Liars."

Of course she didn't mean to offend anyone or truly think they are purposely lying. What she meant was what we often think what we want is not truly what we want. How can that be?

When I was coaching my clients, they often had no problem telling me what problems and challenges they encountered in their lives. It was often very fluent like a speech they have been preparing for years. But when I asked, "What would you like instead?", often there was this sudden pause, and then they would say, "Good question." Then there was another pause before they started to tell me what they wanted. That was like the speech they hadn't practiced for quite a while, or it was a totally new one that they never thought of and thus unfamiliar and unprepared.

We were all born with a purpose. But before we could create a purposeful life, we had to learn how this linear time-space world runs so that first we can survive. For most people, during the course of learning to survive, they forget their original purpose and instead, surviving becomes their primary motivation for living. Instead of creating a life according to our original purpose, most of us live the rest of our lives to survive better. We focus our attention to things that are dangerous and may threaten our life. We practice so much that we get really good at avoiding danger. But the more we avoid the danger, the more danger comes our way. It becomes the norm of our life to just survive until we are cornered by overwhelming danger.

Now if you remember the quantum collapse theory, you would understand why our lives are filled with unwanted, undesirable, or dangerous realities. It's because our attention, our observation, and our measurement of those dangerous situations collapsed those possibilities into our reality.

You might argue "I never thought of those undesirable things before they happened to me." Or "I saw those terrible things happen to others. Of course I want to make sure they don't happen to me in the future. What's wrong to learn from other's mistakes or our own mistakes?" I totally understand your point. I was raised up with the belief of what the Italian philosopher George Santayana's famous quote says: "Those who cannot remember the past are condemned to repeat it." Or, as it is often rephrased: "Those who cannot learn from history are condemned to repeat it." However, quantum theory seems to point to the opposite.

Yes, you are right. When you were born, things were already happening inside and outside the family that you were born into. And there are special reasons why you were born into that particular family. Your family gave you gifts and prepared you to create your own life later. But undesirable situations in your family were not meant for you to avoid in your future. Those situations were to help you define what you want instead and not for you to focus on those situation per se.

For example, I was born to two great teachers who were loved by their students. This gave me the great gift of learning and teaching. But my parents had a terrible relationship and ended up divorcing after decades of suffering, which also caused physical manifestations. My mom had benign breast plasmacytosis, high blood pressure, hyperthyroid, and a stomach ulcer. My dad died of stomach cancer. At one point in my life, I thought I was doomed to have a stomach ulcer or even cancer and that my marriage was having problems. Deep down I suspected I might end up divorced as well. I was trying to avoid all of those. My focus was those potential dangers. And the more I tried to avoid those, the more they were happening. I was literally feeling stomachache and when I was studying pathology at medical school, I can vividly picture what was going on in my body. That was the time I felt sick the most. And to make matters worse, I was having arguments and fight with my husband almost every day or every other day, just like my parents. Worst of all, my children started to suffer as I was suffering from my parents' broken marriage and relationship. My son went into depression for a period when he needed my love and attention the most. Only years later, after I read so many books and trained as a life coach, did I realize that I created all of those things in my life just because I mistook the purpose and message of why I was born to my parents. I began to change my perspective of thinking. Instead of thinking I am going to be as sick as my parents, or that my marriage is going to be as bad as my parents', I start to think, "What did they want instead?" or more importantly, "What did I want?"

That is when things begin to change. I wanted a healthy body and a loving relationship. This may sounds obvious but this change of perspective made a huge difference. This little switch of perspective is just like the light switch. A little and simple flick turns the light on. Until that switch is flicked, that room could be in the darkness for thousands of years. This is when you are quantum collapsing the desired possibilities into your reality. By the time I turned fifty, I had a healthy body, and my husband was telling his parents that our marriage couldn't be better. My son was no longer depressed and we started to see more and more smiles on his face and more confidence in him. My daughter was getting straight As and had already published two novels by age of thirteen. And she is the sweetest angel in the home. My relation with my mom and in-laws was at the best I can remember.

So knowing what you want is about shifting your purpose from surviving or avoiding danger to the purpose of deliberate creating what you want.

In addition to discovering what we want instead from the things we don't like in our current job, another important thing I want you to think about is what you liked in your current job. Most people have a hard time quitting their medical career because they believe they will lose all the things they like if they switched to a different career – the lucrative pay check, the social status, and the power to revive people's lives. When I coach my clients, I often ask them, "What if you don't have to lose all that you like? What if you can keep all of them and get even better?" I can almost see the whole room light up when this question is asked. This is when their eyes glow and they change their posture to sitting tall, wearing a big smile of belief.

I want you to know that this is not just an entertaining thought. This is your way of creating your new career. Yes, you get to choose and keep all your likes. Just like you go to an all-you-can-eat buffet. You never see a sign that says, "If you choose dish A, you cannot choose dish B." or "If you choose dish A, you have to choose dish C." So, if you don't like dish C and love dish A and B, once you pick dish A, you have to live with dish C and sacrifice dish B. That buffet will be out of business the next day. The beauty of an all-you-can-eat buffet is the total freedom of choices and the more diverse the dishes, the better the buffet. So as with life, you have career choices.

All-You-Can-Want Buffet

So the second part of this step is to create an "All-You-Can-Want" Buffet menu. To do that, you want to first make a list of things that you like and want to continue to have. For the things you don't like, flip them to what you would like instead in your future career. You want to list things that you were not able to do with your current medical career, but that you really want to do in the future career. At this point, you don't want to worry about what your new career should be or could be. You just need to list everything you want. Remember there is no limit for the possibilities of what you can have, be, or do. The universe has unlimited resources and possibilities. Things do not happen to you. They are happening for you. You are in charge of the wanting and choosing part. Here is an example of what I would've listed at the time when I wasn't sure if I should quit or not.

	My Current Medical Career	My Future Career
Things I like in my current career that I want to keep in my future career	• Teaching • Mentoring • Coaching • Training • Give seminars & talks • Flexible time • Make my family proud • Role model for my children	
Things I don't like in my current medical career and what I want instead in my future career	• Not addressing the root cause of people's suffering • Lack of financial freedom • Lack of personnel support • Administrative paperwork • Have to seek social approval (grant and manuscript reviewers) • Publish or perish	• Be able to address the root cause of people's suffering • Financial security and freedom • Full administrative support • Teamwork with like-minded and brilliant people • Independent entrepreneur

Things I could not be done in my current career, but I will be able to do in my future career	• Work with cells and animals • Work with hypothesis • Need protocol approval to test hypothesis • Take years to test one hypothesis • Take decades to study in humans • Take another decade to get FDA approval before get to the patient	• Directly work with clients • Total freedom of program design

After you list the things that you would like to have in your new career, then consider in what kind of career you would like to have all these weaved into it. But before you can do that, there is an extremely important step you have to pass. That is to reclaim your purpose.

By this time, you have experienced, learned, and practiced a lot of life skills that have helped you survive. During the process, this knowledge and these skills often get in the way of you discovering the true purpose you were born to fulfill in this life. Now to reclaim the purpose you were born to, it often takes an onion-peeling process, where you have to peel away the beliefs, knowledge, and skills you are so attached to. It usually takes some deep coaching with a masterful life coach. However, during my coaching sessions, I have developed a faster, shorter way to interview. When I was either interviewing people for this book or helping promote my clients' coaching businesses, many clients told me the interviewing process helped them to realize something they never knew before. That happens after they went back to watch the interview a couple of times where they joyfully discovered their purpose, their perfect business niche, and the answer to their burning life question, all within their own answers.

One of my favorite interview questions to my clients is "Fast-forward to your deathbed, when you are leaving this life, what you have to do in your life in order to make you feel at peace and complete at that time so that you can say, "I had a good life. I am fulfilled and I can leave now." I really enjoy the long pauses and a deep breath my clients take after this question, which is then followed by the most inspirational speech of their time.

If you work with me, I would interview you with the following additional questions and film your answers and have you watch them couple of times afterward. The key about the person who interviews you is that they have to be non-judgmental. Avoid someone who knows you too well and has already formed an opinion of you. The interviewer has to love you as you are and be curious about what you would say with no judgment and can refrain from the urge to comment or advise. Here is one of the fun interview exercises I often do with my clients. This exercise helps you to determine your purpose and a career that supports the purpose that you still remember from when you were little. Here are the questions:

1. When you were a child, what profession did you want to do when you were a grown up?
2. What did you like about that?
3. What was a skill you mastered? (hint it can be an imaginary skill!)
4. What's your mantra?

5. How does that mantra make you feel?
6. What are three adjectives people would describe you as? (i.e. nice, smart, and cool)
7. What was the coolest thing you ever heard someone say about you?
8. What are you proud to know about your current job?
9. Pick a fun/powerful word to describe yourself.
10. In a few words, what was a powerful turning point for you?
11. Name your biggest idol.
12. What is a quality of theirs that you admire?
13. What type of coach are you?
14. Pick a descriptive noun that makes you feel joy. (i.e. fantastic, lovely, fun)

After you watch the interview recording, fill in the following paragraph using the answers to each question.

"Ever since I was little, I wanted to be a (1)_____ because of my passion about (2) _____and my ability to naturally (3)_____.

If I had the ability to forever embody (4)_____ I would definitely feel (5)_____.

Everyone tells me that I am (6A)_____ (6B) _____, and (6C) _____. Sometimes I even get told that I possess the ability to (7) _____.

Personally, I am thrilled about my knowledge about (8)

_____.

I seriously am (9) _____.

When I (10) _____ that was the moment I realized that "I got this! And I can do anything!"

If (11) _____met me, we would find that we have (12) _____ in common.

Yup, I'd say I am proud to be a (13) _____. It's really, truly (14) _____!!!"

If you are following through, you should have an "All-You-Can-Want list and a paragraph showing your true purpose. You probably had a couple of ideas of what your future career would be. You can list them in your notebook. Don't worry if you haven't had a clear specific career choice in mind, in which case, you can write down this question in your notebook instead, "What kind of career path will meet the "All-You-Can-Want" list and also fulfill my purpose?" Then you want to put your notebook at your bedside and sleep on it. The next morning, before you get out of bed, be aware of any thoughts or dreams you have had that are messages to help you validate or specify some of choices on your list.

By this time, you should have a pretty clear idea of what career path will fulfill your true purpose.

Your Body Doesn't Lie

If you had more than one choice and you cannot decide, I would very much like to guide you through the process of muscle testing. If you recall in chapter 3, I mentioned the amazing process of muscle testing. You can learn more about muscle testing from Dr. Bruce H. Lipton's book *The Biology of Belief,* Dr. John Diamond's book, *Your Body Doesn't Lie* and Dr. David Hawkins' book, *Power Vs. Force.* The version I often practice with my client as well as myself, is to write down on a piece of paper the choices that you couldn't decide on, then fold the paper so you won't know which one is which. In order to do the test, you will need someone who believes in and shares the value of muscle testing or a professional coach. Before the testing, you would need to measure the baseline strength of your muscle. Usually it is the dominant arm. You raise that arm stretching in front of you at a right angle relative to your body. You would make a positive statement by simply saying your name or just "Yes." Your tester will try to push your arm down while it is raised. That strength is your baseline. Then you would test the negative control by simply making a false statement by simply saying a made-up name or "No." You will experience the weakness of your muscle. Your tester will have an easier time pushing your arm down. You will feel that your logical mind can no longer control your arm even though you still want to keep it at that height. It seems your muscle has its own mind. If you experience this, then you know you are doing it right and you are ready for the test. Now, in your non-dominant hand, hold one of the pieces of paper of the career choices you wrote down, then test the dominant arm again. This time you make the statement "I am holding the career path choice that supports my purpose of this life." Compare the muscle strength of all the choices you have. The strongest one is what your body or inner being agrees with you on at this moment.

One thing you have to know is that you may want something but at that moment your body might "disagree." Just like I mentioned during the workshop, every coach wanted to be a six-figure coach, but their body muscle disagreed. Not because this is the wrong career choice. But because your mindset has not shifted enough to create the physiology that matches what you want. For example, most entrepreneurs want to be a millionaire. But less than 10% of them would become millionaires. That is the 10% who has the right mindset long before they become a millionaire.

If your muscle is weak in responding to your statement but you really want that statement to be true, rest assured we could work together to practice the mindset so that it will match your desired future during the rest of the process.

If you have any questions regarding this step of the process or want me to work with you, I can be reached by email support@ hoeholisticwellness.com.

Notes

_____

_____

_____

_____

_____

_____

_____

_____

_____

_____

_____

_____

_____

_____

_____

_____

_____

_____

_____

Chapter 6

Step 3: L for Leverage

(Leverage Your Gift and Turn Quitting into Upgrading)

"Life is a series of natural and spontaneous changes. Don't resist them; that only creates sorrow. Let reality be reality. Let things flow naturally forward in whatever way they like."
– Lao Tzu

Will I Find a Better Job?

There was once a traveler passing a village. He saw an elder outside the village. He was eager to ask, "Hello there. I am looking for a place to live. Could you tell me if this village is a good place? What sort of people lives here?"

The elder slowly raised his eyes and asked, "Oh, hello. Where are you from? How was the place you came from? What sort of people lived there?"

73

"To be honest, it was a horrible place." The traveler replied shaking his head. "People there were selfish, lazy, and not trustworthy. I am so glad I am leaving there. I can't wait to find a better place to live. So, tell me how is your village?"

"Is that so?" replied the elder. "Well, I'm afraid our village is no different."

Disappointed, the traveler continued on his way. Soon after, another stranger walked upon the village, greeting the elder, "Good afternoon," he then asked, "I am looking for a place to stay for a few days. Would it be a good idea to look for a place in your village? Are people here nice and friendly?" "Oh, hi, there." The elder looked at him, "How is the place you are from? What sort of people was there?" Tears coming down from the young traveler's eyes, "I miss my hometown so much! They were the sweetest people in the world. They were nice, honest, warmhearted, and hardworking. I can't wait to go back after my business is done." "Well," the elder said, "No worry, you will find the same nice, honest, and hardworking people in our village." "I am so glad to hear! I have been so lucky meeting nice people all my way!" Thanking the elder, the young traveler joyfully walked into the village. Another villager overheard the two conversations and was confused and asked the elder, "Why did you say we were bad people to the first traveler and nice people to the second traveler?" The elder smiled...

You probably heard some version of the same story. I don't remember when and where I heard this story. But this is my version of the inspiration and reminder for a self-check whenever I want to move away from something. I have to do many adjustments to make sure I will not end up in the same situation. That is also why I created the coaching program to help my clients to clean up their thoughts, beliefs, and energies carried over from their previous version of life so that they can totally upgrade to the next version. In this chapter, I will guide you through step 3 of the process, turning quitting into upgrading.

The process of managing and clearing out those frustrations is an important step of the process. Why? Our emotions are our messengers. The more intense the emotion, the bigger the message. If not managed or cleared, the thoughts and beliefs beneath that emotion will come up again and again no matter what new career you choose. Therefore, it is important to address them before you quit your current job so that they won't keep hunting you.

To help clean up any frustrations you have about your current job, fill in the first column of the table below with anything or anyone that triggers your feeling of frustration. In the second column, fill in what format this might show up in your future career. In the third column, fill in your answer to the question, "What if those people or things that frustrated you in your current job were actually necessary to prepare you for a better career? If so, in what way did they help you?" In the forth column, fill in your answer to the question, "If you improve in this area, what will your future career look like?"

People or Things That Frustrated Me	Could This Show Up in My New Career? In What Form?	What If They Were Actually Preparing Me for a Better Career? How Did They Help Me?	If I Improve, What Will People or Things Look Like in My New Career
Example 1: Those reviewers of my research grant proposal and manuscripts, who didn't understand what I was talking about and gave bad comments.	Example 1: People might not understand my business proposal or client might misunderstand what service I am providing and complain that they didn't get what they expected.	Example 1: The misunderstanding of the reviewers helps me to improve my communication skills. When I write or speak, I will keep the audience in my mind and connect with them to build mutual understanding.	Example 1: My business investors will understand my proposal. My clients will have the appropriate expectations of the service I provide and be happy about the great results they get.
Example 2: I hate the tedious animal protocol application process and the confusing software platform.	Example 2: The annual report, financial booking, tax filing, legal documents etc. Could be all tedious for a small business entrepreneur.	Example 2: These works help me to better plan my business and learn to delegate tasks and include in my business budget.	Example 2: I will free myself from these tasks and provide business opportunities to others who love to do these jobs.

Your turn here	Your turn here	Your turn here	Your turn here
Your turn here	Your turn here	Your turn here	Your turn here

Am I a Loser?

The second important belief we need to clean up at this step is the negative image associated with "quitting."

A friend of mine went to a parent event at Harvard University. The host asked all the parents, "Who is still doing what you think you would do when you were 18?" Only a few hands went up. About 90% of the parents were not doing what they thought they wanted to do. My friend who has been working in the biotech company for decades told me later that he was very surprised to see so many other parents actually switched their career paths. To him, quitting a job was mostly associated with a negative image. It is true that sometimes quitting means giving up prematurely. However, there is a huge difference between me at eighteen years old and forty-eight years old. If you are thinking of quitting your medical career at age forty-eight, it is unlikely you are talking about quitting lightly.

Because this is a big decision, it is usually associated with intense frustration and doubts. Each individual may have different thoughts that trigger the frustration around quitting their medical job. But after I interviewed many who have gone through the process, I found the following beliefs were quite common.

Myth #1: "Quitting is a sign of lack of courage, determination, and perseverance."

Yes, the stigma of quitting is associated with the lack of courage, determination, and perseverance. But most likely, quitting your medical career is the opposite of those. It actually takes courage and determination to quit an honorable career in the medical field, and it also takes perseverance to embark on a new career path.

You see, after you reclaimed your life purpose, and after we cleaned up the energy using the above exercise, you are not running away from something you don't like. You are graduating from the previous job and upgrading it to a higher level that better serves your true purpose. To achieve this, you are gathering your courage and determination. This is not really "quitting." This is a strategic "letting go" and upgrading.

Myth #2: "As medical professionals, we are supposed to sacrifice our own lives to save others."

This is a big one. Yes, another stigma of quitting is associated with selfishness or fear of sacrifice. However, quitting a medical career due to the burnout and severe work-life imbalance is a strategic move. Sacrifice is virtuous but not always necessary and, at times, may cause chronic-fatigue-related medical accidents and malpractice. There are actually many scientific studies on this topic.

Recently, during a spring body-mind-spirit cleanse coaching, I was discussing with my clients how overuse of antibiotics in the food industry and at the hospital has caused many problems. But one cause of the overuse of antibiotics in the hospitals was very unexpected. In a 2014 study published in the *Journal of the American Medical Association* (JAMA), researchers tracked 21,867 hospital visits to 204 doctors in 23 different practices and found that doctors prescribed more antibiotics when they worked longer shifts. After merely four hours of working, there was an increase in antibiotic prescriptions given to patients – whether they were needed or not. This is termed decision-fatigue.

This is just one of many examples of how the wellbeing of a healthcare professional can affect the quality of the service.

I see sacrifice as a version of investment. That means, when we sacrifice our health, relationship, family, it will only be worth the investment if the outcome is way more grand than our wellbeing, for example many more lives will be saved or improved. However, if after we sacrifice our own wellbeing, our patients are not saved nor improved as much and instead, our quality of service to them is lowered because of our less optimal wellbeing, then it is not a good investment. It will then be a good time to re-evaluate your career. For example, when you are burnt-out, your patients no longer receive the top-quality care from you; or your research is aimed to survive and sustain the job and no longer about creativity and discovery. This is when you know it is time for a big change. This is an individual decision, a decision to be made without being judged neither by others nor by yourself as a right or wrong decision. It is a wanted or unwanted-type of decision.

The best gift you can give to your loved ones and this world is you being happy and healthy. What you can do from that place of happiness and health is what the world needs the most. From a place of discontent and burnout, there is not much you can give. Therefore, never sacrifice your happiness and health for anything. Instead of sacrifice, a true hero would find creative ways to save both his/her own life and others.

Confucius is one of the greatest teachers in ancient China. He emphasized children respecting and obeying their parents. A lot of his disciples, and some modern-day people, have over interpreted his teachings. Once, one of his pupils proudly told him that when his father was angry with him and beating him badly, he just knelt and let him. He expected Confucius would praise his filial piety. "You fool! Why didn't you run?" Confucius scolded him. "If your father was too angry and beat you to death, he would be heartbroken and regret for the rest of his life."

So you see, just like that pupil, letting his father beat him badly was not a virtue. Running away was a strategy not an act of losing or being disrespectful. Quitting a medical career that is hurting you is not an act of weakness. If we were chronically burnt-out, stressed, overwhelmed, had no quality time for family and friends, who would benefit from us?

The current biomedical research and healthcare systems have many non-sustainable systemic flaws that will continue to cause tension and stress among researchers and physicians. If these are negatively affecting your health, your family's wellbeing, and your ability to serve patients from the best version of you, then exploring opportunities outside of the system where you can fulfill your servant's purpose is not only not a disgrace but a brilliant move.

Myth #3: "It was a big mistake and waste with so many years of investment of time and money."

When I was in high school, my mom took me to take a personality test designed for finding out what career was suitable. My results indicated that I was suitable to study management and public health. But at that time, I had no idea what management and public health were about. We ended up not taking the advice. My mom let me take what was popular at that time, English for Science and Technology in the foreign language department. The language part prepared me to later come to the US. The science part later prepared me to become a biomedical researcher. If I took the management and public health major, things would've been very different. Nothing that happened in my life was a mistake. Everything happened for me and prepared me to move to the next step. I learned so much by being a professor and immuno-oncology researcher for almost two decades. There are so many things in this career that I treasure. But moving on to be a life coach is the next step in my path. Those skills I learned during my medical career were not wasted. They all prepared me for success in the next job. All the people who I interviewed who transitioned from medical professionals to health/life coaches said that their previous medical profession prepared them and inspired them for their next career move and was not a waste nor a mistake.

If I never lived both the joy and frustration of my medical career, I would not be writing this book. I would have no way to know life coaching would be my way of serving my life purpose. Instead of a waste, my medical career was an essential step in my search of my purpose.

Myth #4: "Why I am feeling so uncomfortable when just thinking about quitting. It is too overwhelming. Does this signal a wrong direction to move?"

Life is like climbing the stairs except that each step takes so long that after a while you forget you are just on one of the steps and it feels as if you are at a permanent position. When it's time to climb to the next step, you've become so used to the current step and fear of the unknown and fear of losing what you had on the current step.

You are uncomfortable but it is not because you made a bad career choice. It's because you reached a place:

- The edge of your comfort zone. It's breakthrough time!
- The end of your stair step. It's level up time!
- Computer crashing phase. It's upgrade time!

When I was trained at the Health Coach Institute, my coach always reminded us that "It is ok to feel ok." At first, I had a hard time understanding the significance of this statement. Soon I came to realize how important it is to feel ok. The part of us that is in charge of survival is always looking for danger, for "not-ok". It is like a security guard whose job is looking for something wrong. If everything is ok, that part would be "out of a job" at least it feels that way. So when everything is ok, it feels strangely dangerous. That feeling prevents you from being totally ok. On the plus side, by not being totally ok, any problems and issues that arise as a result can always be used as motivation. In other words, when things are going badly, part of us is actually happy about it. Imagine that part says, "Oh, my, at least I know it very well. I've been trained for that. I've been looking for that. I am so familiar with things going bad. If things are going well, I will feel strange or even threatened. I feel excited and secure when things are going bad."

Most people associate fear with failure. Not many people know that fear is in many cases associated with success. Because we practiced paying attention to what bad things could happen so much, thanks to our survival system, we get used to preparing for the worst. But as we rarely prepare for the best, being successful is not as familiar as failure. And when we are not familiar with what success feels like, we fear it.

Do you remember when you were preparing for an exam or a competition, you might've heard the saying, "Prepare for the worst and aim for the best."? But in reality, 90% of the people spend 90% of their time preparing for the worst. And only 10% of the people spend their 90% of the time preparing for the best. What's the success rate? You guessed it! When the results of your exam and competition were revealed, for most people, it feels like a big relief that the results were pretty much as they expected. That feeling of relief kept them going and repeating their future life events again and again. Breaking through the pattern as you are doing now by quitting is way more uncomfortable than the relief of seeing the expected results, even if the results show failure or mediocrity.

That's why when you decide to quit your current medical career and move on to be a successful entrepreneur or some other new adventure, it definitely feels scary to that survival part of your brain. That's what your emotions are about.

After cleaning up your beliefs and turning all negative thoughts about your job and the possibility of quitting into appreciative thoughts, you are now ready to move on to the next step, to build your vision and say yes to the bravest version of yourself.

If you have any questions or want me to guide you through the process, I can be reached at support@hoeholisticwellness.com.

Notes

Chapter 7

Step 4: E for Envision

(Build Your Unique Vision, and Say, "Yes, I Am Coming.")

"What you think, you become; What you feel, you attract;
What you imagine, you create."
– Buddha

Life Is a VR Game

Both of my parents were excellent teachers. My father was a professor at a law school and my mother was a middle school language teacher. They were always rated high in their teaching profession and both were loved by their institute and students. When many told me that I was a really good teacher, I attributed this to my parents. But there is one gift I was born with has particularly helped me. After I prepared my teaching material, I ran the whole thing over in my head many times before the class. I was not just trying to memorize the material.

I was having a vivid 3D virtual reality (VR) experience in my mind. I could see the classroom, my students, the projector, and the screen. As I mentally visited the classroom, I could see myself standing there teaching and the students responding. I could sense their feelings and my feelings. When I physically went to the classroom to teach, things often went smoothly just like I had imagined. This happened beautifully when I went to present my research in an international conference in Japan for the first time. I had just started my career and I thought I was going to be very nervous in front of more than 200 top scientists from all over the world. I habitually ran over the presentation in my head many times before the conference. When I stood there, I was surprised by how calm I was and how fluent and confident I was. I was totally in the zone. Later, I was approached by many scientists who were fascinated by my research, which to me was nothing comparing to what they were doing. But the presentation was effective in getting everyone interested. Even my mentor was amazed at how calm I was. No one knew the whole thing was in my mind before it happened.

This gift came so naturally that I never gave too much thought to it nor did I talk about it to anyone until I read an article about visualization and mental rehearsal.

Mental rehearsal has been a widely used psychological technique to enhance the performance of athletes and musicians.

In a research reported in 2004 in the *Journal of Cognitive Brain Research*, twelve piano students with the same level of piano skills and learning capacity were measured by functional magnetic resonance imaging (fMRI). The MRI scan showed similar regions of the brain lit up when the students were physically playing the piano and when the students were reading the notes and mentally playing the piano without any movement.

More interestingly, in a 2018 issue of the *Neuron*, a study by Stanford University showed, for the first time, that you could teach a monkey to move a cursor on a computer screen without physical movement of the arm. In their study, a monkey was connected to a brain-machine-interface (BMI) device, which instructed the brain, similar to a human mental rehearsal, to move a cursor on a screen without any physical movement of the arm. The experiment did for the first time prove in real time that a monkey could learn a task he never knew before and later physically perform the new skill and even adapt to variations of the task. That's how powerful mental imagery is.

What these experiments showed us is that mental imagery is as powerful as action, at least in the process of learning as tested in these reports. Now what has that to do with your quitting your medical career and building your future career? What I am about to tell you is that it is not only powerful in learning, but also powerful in planning and realizing your dream life.

Time Travel and Wisdom "Thief"

In my coaching program, I use mental rehearsal not for learning or practicing any skills, but rather to help my clients "time travel" to the future to tap into the wisdom of the future version of my client. This whole process also helps my clients to "wave collapse" their desired future possibility into reality. As we discussed before, our materialized "reality" is just like the particle-form of light. It is a result of our observation. Without our observation, light exists as formless energy. The attention we give to certain possibilities of our life during our mental rehearsal will bring that into the material world.

Through various versions of mental rehearsal, I have helped my clients to achieve otherwise stressful tasks like purchasing their first house, getting pregnant despite medical conditions, mending hard relationships, landing their dream job, etc. with ease and peace of mind.

I also personally experienced the power of mental rehearsal coaching to transform my own fear and my reality. When my coach encouraged me to do Facebook Live to let people know about my coaching business, I was surprised to find how much fear I had. As a perfectionist at that time, I just couldn't get myself comfortable around the idea doing a live video to expose myself in front of the world not even knowing who would see me and what they would think of me. I struggled with the idea for more than a year until I attended a coaching event, I was guided to visualize the bravest version of myself in the future when I was comfortable with Facebook Live and connected to the people who needed my help. Then I wrote a letter to the future me at three months away. That was how much time I decided that I needed to conquer the fear and establish a Facebook Live series to introduce my coaching. In the letter, I described my fear at that time and how I admired the courage and achievement of the future me. I vividly imagined the experience that future me would have. Then the letter was sealed, addressed to myself with a stamp. It was kept by my coach to send to me in three months.

Our time is linear and seems fixed in length. But our feeling of time varies. Those three months went fast and yet was long enough for me to totally forget about the letter and its contents. But then one day the letter arrived in my mailbox. I was excited to open the letter from the "past me". Imagine that! It is a very strange moment as if time and space were not linear and continuous, and I was reading from someone else's letter to the "now me". It was the dear "past me" who was frustrated and struggling with the idea of doing Facebook Live. That feeling of fear was so foreign to the "now me" reading the letter. At this time, I have already finished season one of the live series, which is known by hundreds of people if not more. I also started season two of the series. I feel so free and easy and when I have an idea I just hop into my little studio and start live recording. I don't need scripts nor the worry of what to wear or if my hair is right. This was unthinkable for the "past me" three months ago. That's how mental rehearsal is so powerful if combined with life coaching. It literally creates the reality you desire.

Dear Xuemei:

I am here thanking you for sneaking in the idea of the Pajama Talk. That's the best 50th BD birthday gift I received! No one on earth knows me better than you, my future you.

I will live through the empowerment to meet you in 90 days. So we can enjoy the milestones of the mission we set out to do together. To touch the hearts that are ready to awake and open to transformation and create beautiful lives on earth.

While you are reading this letter, you know you have passed all the fears and obstacles I am experiencing now. You are at a better place coaching a lot of clients and changing their lifes. Congratulations!

I love you so much. I am here for you knowing you are there waiting for me.

Yours always
Xuemei in your memory

I also use a modified version of mental rehearsal for my own archery practice. As a member of an archery team, we are expected to practice three to four days a week to maintain our skill level, and more time than that if we want to improve. As much as I love archery and want to improve my score, I just can't commit that much time to practice. One night I was watching a world archery tournament on YouTube. I was so into it as if I was the world #1 archer in the event. While I was watching, I could almost feel what the archer was feeling and thinking as if I was in her mind. My heart was beating as her heart. My arm was in her arm. My fingers were in her fingers. Before she released the arrow, I could predict where the arrow was going to land on the target. Just watching the event in this way, it literally became a mental simulation for me. I loved watching the world archery event so much that I began to watch one YouTube archery event every day for the next three to four weeks until I finished all the clips I could find. Then magic happened. My archery score improved without me committing more practice time in the range. What is even more interesting is that while I was in the tournament, every time I raised my bow, one of the world best archers I watched on YouTube would come alive in my mind and I would almost become that person and so my scores improved.

Now this is how I want you to envision your future success.

By this time, if you have been following the first three steps, you should have already reclaimed your life purpose and cleared many beliefs that no longer support your purpose. Based upon these, this step is to use mental rehearsal to paint a detailed picture of the future you.

There are many ways to do a mental rehearsal. My clients' favorite one is when I guide them through a mental rehearsal meditation to bring them to their future with their current issues. When they envision the future seeing how their issue was already resolved, they often felt relieved, inspired, and empowered. When they came back to the present, they got their solutions to their current problems and were amazed by the process.

But the guided meditation is not suitable to do by reading this book. However, a letter to the future you will be just as powerful.

A Letter to the Future You

Here is how you will write the letter in the following order:

1. Define how much time you would need to quit your job and/or develop a new career. This will be the future you you want to write to. For example, if you want to quit your job within a year, and you want to know how your life would be in alignment with your purpose and desires you worked out in the first three steps, the future you that you want to write to would be the you twelve months from now.

2. List problems and issues that are currently preventing you from making the decision from moving forward to establish a new career, and any confusions that need to be clarified. In your letter, you would describe these and ask the future you for advice.

3. In your mind's eye, what would life look like in the future?
   - What job would you have?
   - What would you be doing for yourself?
   - What would you be doing for others?

- What do you look like?
- What clothes do you wear?
- What do you hear?
- What do you see?
- How do you feel?
- What house do you live in?
- What car do you drive?
- What food do you eat?
- Who is with you?
- Anything else you can see...

When you picture these, bear in mind that you can have, be, or do anything in the mental rehearsal. There is no limit, not even the sky is your limit. In your letter, describe your desired future and acknowledge that the future you is experiencing all of these. Then describe your feeling about that. Think about it, all these will be happening in the future thanks to what you are working on right now. Are you proud of yourself now?

1. Thank future you for any advice you need and congratulate future you, experiencing the desired future you are building today.
2. Once you have a full description of the life the future you will experience, ask yourself this question, "What does the future you have to believe in order for him/her to experience that life?" Write down your answer on a separate piece of paper for later use.
3. After you sign the letter, seal it in a colorful envelope with your address and stamp.
4. Give this letter to a friend, not someone who lives with you. Tell your friend to send this letter to you on the

date you specify, say twelve months from now. Make sure your friend has this task on his/her calendar so they won't forget.

5. Now by this time, your future is built!

If you have any questions or would like to be guided through the process, I can be reached at: support@hoeholisticwellness.com

Notes

_____

_____

_____

_____

_____

_____

_____

_____

_____

_____

_____

_____

_____

_____

_____

_____

_____

_____

Chapter 8

Step 5: V for Voice

(Removing Roadblocks by Giving the Parts of Internal Conflicts Their Voices)

"Your cork will always float unless
you are holding it down."
– Abraham-Hicks

What Could Go Wrong with This Decision?

If you are following each step, by this time, you have reclaimed your purpose and know exactly you want, and have "visited" your future life and had a conversation with your future self by writing a letter. How does that feel?

There are still three more steps to make sure you will wave collapse the reality as we planned so far.

One of the paradigms of the transformational coaching method I adopt is, "If it is ok to have it, you would already have it." Meaning, if you are struggling to get what you desire or it seems like it is taking forever for what you desire to come to you, then some parts of you must believe it is not ok to have what you desire.

Many people question the idea of "Ask, and it shall be given." One of the reasons that people do not receive what they asked for is that parts of them ask for different, sometimes opposite, things, which I call "internal conflict." In this chapter, we will talk about how to turn internal conflict into internal harmony so that your asking becomes unanimous and then you shall receive.

How Is Your Relationship with Money?

My biggest struggle around quitting my medical school job is money. I know I love coaching. Coaching my clients made me alive, and I am really good at it. But I have a problem asking for money or receiving money for the work I do. I struggle a lot and not sure if I can still make enough money if I quit and work as a life coach.

During a training event, we learned that our relationship with money is a mirror of your marriage relationship. That suddenly opened up my eyes. I can see my relationship with my husband and understand why money is not coming my way as I needed. There is a part of me that is refusing the money. It is an internal conflict I have been holding and I hadn't realized.

There is a part of me that is so independent that seeking help is out of the picture. There's another part that is humble and willing to accept help. But these two parts are not playing equal. I have been favoring one and neglecting the other. My independent part has been dominant throughout my life until this point. My mom raised me up all by herself while my father was working in a different state and only visiting home twice a year and not providing much financial support. Probably, in my mind, women in the family are supposed to be strong and take care of the family finances and raise children along with doing all the household stuff. That was my childhood image of marriage and family. Since my mother was teaching at an elementary school and later at a middle school, both two to three hours away from home, I was sent to daycare when I was very little. I remember one day my arm was dislocated by someone on the daycare staff when she was lifting me by the arm and my mom could not pick me up until late in the day. I was in pain but was scared to tell the staff. I was so little but I had to wait the whole day with pain until my mom arrived. Things like that made me very strong and independent. I had to deal with everything in my life without help. My parents sent me to boarding school for both my middle and high school. I had to take care of myself without help from my parents. In my mind, doing everything by myself was so natural and I was so good at most of the things I did. I had good grades at school. I remember I took fifteen courses in one semester in college and graduated with two majors. One in English and one in Biochemistry. Since I could figure out most things by myself, I rarely asked for help or for permission.

When I got married, I didn't realize my independency was going to be a problem. I secretly wanted my husband to be able to support the whole family, but I didn't trust that he could provide the financial security. My images of childhood likely created the reality that my husband would not bring financial security to the family as my father did. That was never a big problem until my husband transitioned to have his own startup biotech company. I was so frightened that I could imagine that we would be broke, unable to afford the mortgage, and possibly become homeless soon. That was a crazily frightening period and the lowest point of our marriage. But on the other hand,

I was proud to be the only breadwinner during that period. I am too independent. I often decided things without asking my husband's permission. Meanwhile, my husband was too busy to care what I decided. He trusted me. Things always worked out perfectly until I wanted to quit my job and become a life coach.

Wanting to quit my job at the medical school put me in a vulnerable position where I needed money to support my transition. Even though, my husband's startup had not taken off yet, he was able to secure enough funding to support the family and me. This was not what I was used to. To make matters worse, this time, I began to worry if I was going to make enough money by coaching. The more I worried, the harder it became to quit my job, which meant I was making less from coaching, and doubting even more if coaching was the right direction forward. And you can see where this spiral was going. These beliefs of "independency" and "I can do everything by myself without help" became a roadblock in my path to pursue my dreams and purpose. Without removing them, the internal conflict would be there making every step of the way heavier and harder than necessary.

My internal conflict was such that one part of me would want to ask for money to help me move onto the new career. The other part of me would be ashamed and would want to continue the past structure of the marriage and finances. Basically, one part of me wanted to stay at the old job and remain independent and dominant. The other part wanted to quit and realize my dream of becoming a full-time life coach.

There was a part of me that was objecting to the success of my coaching business. For my coaching business to thrive and for me to quit my job, I had to resolve this internal conflict.

Turning Internal Conflicts into Creativity

So before we move on to how to resolve internal conflict, let's first find out what is your internal conflict around quitting your current medical career by answering the following questions.

- Were there two parts of you, one wanting to quit and the other wanting to stay?
- What are the hidden reasons for each part?
- Is it about money?
- Is it about family support?
- Is it about leaving things or people you love?
- Is it about responsibilities?
- Is it about pride?
- Is it about confidence?
- What other conflict could it be?

Once my clients identify their two internal conflicts, I guide them through one of my clients' all-time favorite exercises. It's called "parts work" and it serves to resolve the internal conflicts. During the exercise I would first assign each of the two parts of the conflict to one of my client's hand with a name or a symbol. Then we would acknowledge that both parts have good intentions and thank the parts for doing a great job for these intentions (e.g. keeping you safe, etc.). And then, we work with the parts to figure out which methods the parts use that can be upgraded. For example, you might want improve "keeping you safe." We make sure no parts will be fired. They only get promoted. We then work to appreciate all the parts by asking "What would have happened to me if you hadn't been around?" and "What it thinks it might have to teach the other part and to learn from the other part?" After the appreciation and understanding, the magic happens when both parts stated they have no objection to working together in support of your wellbeing as their common goals. This is when I see the creativity come out of my clients. It's when both parts team up to create a better and more efficient way. At the end of the exercise, I would ask my clients to bring both hands close to each other. When the process is successful, it is amazing to see if the two hands close like a magnet. If the appreciation and learning are not complete, the hands will refuse to close.

I still remember when I did my parts work, I was moved to tears. One part was a pair of gigantic white-feathered wings; the other part was some sort of weight that holds down the wings. You might have guessed which part is which. Yes, the wings were the part that wanted me to quit my job at medical school to become a full-time life coach and the weight was the part that wanted me to stay. To my surprise, when these two parts met, they were not trying to argue and convince the other part. They were like old friends and they had been working together to keep me safe, grounded but never letting me lose my purpose and freedom to thrive. After the parts met, they decided to loosen up a little of the weight but cautioned me to be creative about my financial situation and allow my husband to help me and never lose my servant's heart as I thrived with my business. That was the best wisdom I got from my parts!

After you remove your roadblock and transform your internal conflict into internal harmony, you are ready to move onto the next exciting step of the process, taking empowered actions!

I can't wait to hear what messages you received from your inner wisdom through this work. Email me your insights or any questions you have. I can be reached at support@ hoeholisticwellness.com

Notes

_____

_____

_____

_____

_____

_____

_____

_____

_____

_____

_____

_____

_____

_____

_____

_____

_____

_____

_____

Chapter 9

Step 6: E for Empower

(Take Only Empowered Action)

*"Choose a job you love, and you will
never have to work a day in your life."*
– Confucius

How Can I Move Forward Without Regrets?

Bronnie Ware is an Australian nurse who collected the last epiphanies of her dying patients and wrote an inspiring blog titled *Regrets of the Dying*. The 2009 blog reached 8 million readers by 2012 when Bronnie decided to turn the blog into her bestselling memoir, *The Top Five Regrets of the Dying*. Here are the top five regrets in her book:

#1 Regret: "I wish I'd had the courage to live a life true to myself, not the life others expected of me."

#2 Regret: "I wish I hadn't worked so hard."

#3 Regret: "I wish I'd had the courage to express my feelings."

#4 Regret: "I wish I had stayed in touch with my friends."

#5 Regret: "I wish that I had let myself be happier."

In supporting Bronnie's claim, in a research published in the April 2018 issue of *Journal Emotion*, psychologists Tom Gilovich and Shai Davidai reported two types of regrets in human life. One type of regret is ought-related, which is driven by unfulfilled duties and responsibilities. The other type of regret is ideal-related, which is driven by unrealized goals and aspirations. In their report titled "The ideal road not taken: The self-discrepancies involved in people's most enduring regrets," Dr. Gilovich and Dr. Daviai discovered that people are more likely to take action to cope with ought-related regrets than ideal-related regrets. As you can see, the top five regrets reported by Bronnie are mostly ideal-related regrets. In other words, our career life is more likely to be consumed by our duties and responsibilities, leaving no space for our ideas.

Anyone can quit a job and find another one. I know a lot of my friends who went into biotech and the pharmaceutical industry and often moved from one company to another. Every time they moved, they got a better salary and title promotion. This is not the purpose of this book. The reason we took the "pain" to go through these steps is to revolutionize your career by truly connecting your career choice to your purpose, passion, and ideas so that you wouldn't feel you have to work a day in your life. Because you love and you are excited about what you do so much that it doesn't feel like a job, an obligation, or simply breadwinning. And more importantly, when you are on your deathbed, you will not have these top five regrets, which unfortunately a lot of burnt-out medical professionals will have to experience.

You may ask, why it is so important to die without regrets other than feeling bad for a little while before we pass? Simply put, it depends on what death means to you. For people who believe death is the end of the story, then feeling bad at the end just makes a sad story. But some people believe that we are eternal and the physical death is just a transition from physical to non-physical. Our essence and consciousness continues in the non-physical form and will regroup and manifest into physical as the story continues. Therefore, your accomplishments and fulfillment of your life's purpose will have a significant impact on how the story is going to continue.

Regardless what your beliefs are around death, you can at least agree that having those top five regrets at your deathbed is not fun. Look at it this way, it was not easy for you to grow from a single cell, remain in the dark for ten months, painfully come out to this world, survive your environment, and go through all the hardship to get through your medical career. At this crossroad, you are going to decide how the rest of the story is going to be. If your choice is like most people, you end up with, say, the #1 regret: "I wish I'd had the courage to live a life true to myself, not the life others expected of me." It will feel like you spent all your time practicing and faithfully playing a game, which at the end, you realize you got the rules all wrong and you have been scoring for other team. Now at the end of the game, you're eager to start the game all over again to just get it right the next time instead of moving on to the next level of the game. That's not fun.

Ok, now how can we move on with this decision of a career change without having those regrets at the end of our lives?

Why Didn't We Just Do Those Things so We Won't Regret?

We start by asking, why most people didn't get to do these things? If you ask them if these five things are important or not, 100% of them would say yes, otherwise they would not be regretting them on their deathbed. So if everyone knows how important these are, why don't they just do it? The reason is not that they think these are not important or that they never thought of them. Then, what is the reason?

Let's first take a look at Einstein's famous equation:

$$E=MC^2$$

We all know that E is energy, M stands for mass, and C stands for the speed of light. This equation tells us that matter and energy is convertible. But not many people know that this equation is not complete. The more complete equation is the following one, where P is momentum, M_0 is the resting mass.

$$E^2=P^2C^2 + m_0^2 c^4$$

When an object is resting, there is no momentum (P=0). Therefore the equation becomes $E=MC^2$ as P^2C^2 is zero. For any moving object, the energy equals the energy needed for keeping the momentum (P>0) and the energy of the resting mass. You see, in order for an object to move, there has to be extra energy to keep the momentum. This is the same if we want to move beyond the idea phase. We need extra energy to create the momentum.

When we think about an idea for a second and then we forget about it, there is not much energy and momentum built in it. Therefore, the idea remains an idea. However, if we keep thinking about the idea, without being distracted or disrupting it with discouraging thoughts or negative influences, then we keep the momentum rolling like a snowball. Soon this idea will inspire empowered action and manifest into our reality. And the key of building such momentum is getting extra energy and avoiding negative energy.

If you heard about the story of Jesus healing the leper, you might remember that after Jesus healed him, Jesus cautioned him, "See that you don't tell anyone." There were many speculated reasons for that. One of the reasons though, is that you will lose your momentum. There are enough people out there who will question, doubt, and try to use their logic and experience to deny you from where they are. But you are at your place deciding if you want to leap forward. If the people became aware, sooner than you know, you will be convinced to not believe it either and think this must be an illusion or some dark magic. The moment you lose your trust and start to doubt, you lose the momentum and the energy you "borrowed" from your supporters. Just like that leper who borrowed energy from Jesus who was temporally holding the energy for him. Such healing will not sustain unless you keep the momentum going until you are over the hill.

To illustrate this, I often show my clients this imaginary hill they have to get over to achieve their goals. As you can see in this figure (on the following page), the left side of the hill is your current medical career. You were burnt-out, unable to take good care of yourself, disconnected with your family, feeling unfulfilled, wondering if you should quit and find a dream career, but not sure if it's the right choice. On the right side of the hill is your future dream career, where you serve people the best, fulfilling your purpose. You can still take care of yourself so you show up with the best version of yourself as you serve, and you will enjoy the security and freedom with an abundance of resources.

When you are at the left side of the hill, you have your idea and dream. But you also have a lot of fear and doubt weighing you down. They are coming from the beliefs you picked up on your trail of growing up and surviving. These beliefs were good to protect you so you could grow up in a harsh environment. But they have almost done their jobs now. These old beliefs are Gravity 1, which is preventing you or slowing you down from getting over the hill. In order to overcome this gravity to build enough momentum, you will need extra "anti-gravity" support. Someone has good positive energy, who can hold you accountable; kick you in the butt when you are off track, and cheer you on along the way. The climbing process may be slow and laborious or fast and fun, depending on the anti-gravity support you get. Once you get to the top, you have maxed your potential and accumulated enough energy for momentum. You will know when you are on top of the hill. Because at that time, you will have clarity, seeing the big picture and your dream life on the other side becoming so real and so close. You can't wait to ski or fly down the hill to dive into the dream life. At that point, you no longer feel frustrated or hesitant. With a gentle nudge, you will fly. On your way to your dream life, you will speed up with the help of Gravity 2, which are your new upgraded beliefs that support you and are in total alignment with your dream career.

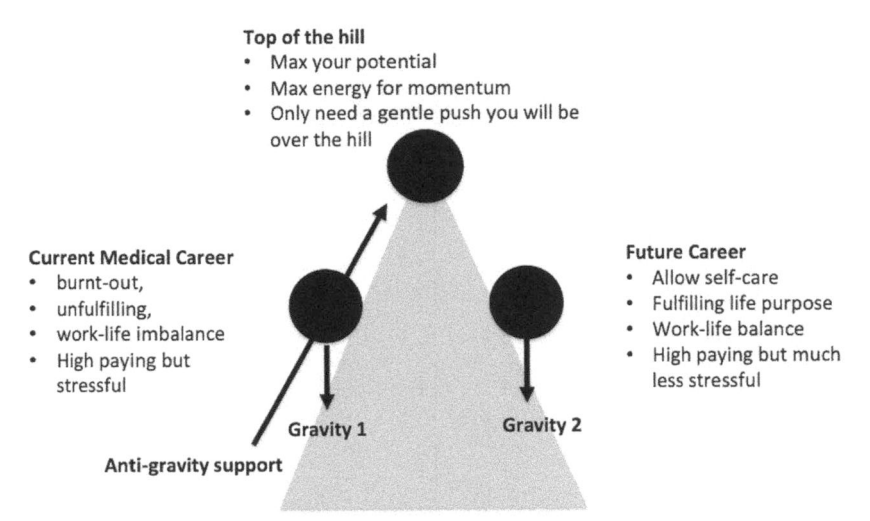

Gravity 1. Is your road block. Some old beliefs you are so use to but is no longer serving your purpose.
Gravity 2. Is your upgraded beliefs that support your purpose and new adventure.

So you see how important it is to keep the momentum going in alignment with what you want to achieve in this life. Many people cannot hold the momentum beyond a few seconds of thought without the extra support of energy. With so much negativity going around in our society, it is much easier to be distracted, talked out of our alignment rather than being supported firmly by someone who shares our vision and can hold the vision and energy for you. So the keys to keeping your momentum are to:

- Identify Gravity 1 beliefs that will keep you from moving forward
- Find your anti-gravity support, the vision-energy holder
- Identify Gravity 2, beliefs that are in alignment with your dream career

Here is a table to help you identify those key elements.

	Belief #1	Belief #2	Belief #3
Gravity 1			
Gravity 2			
	People in my life	Books	Mentors / Coaches
Anti-gravity support			

So yes, if you want to create a career that makes a difference in the world and, at the same time, not have regrets when you die, it is important you learn how to take empowered action and keep the momentum without being distracted and talked out of your alignment.

How to Take Empowered Action?

Action follows an idea. To take empowered action, you first have to empower an idea. How to know if an idea is empowered or not? Take this example, is "Slowdown and have a good plan" an empowered idea? Or is it an impulsive action or an empowered action? The answer is, "It all depends." It depends on the emotion associated with the thought or idea.

For example, when you have an idea, you become so excited about it that the more you think about it, the more great ideas come to your mind. You are thrilled with joy as if you hit the jackpot and have to stop and sort out all the great ideas before you can take the first step. From that joyful place, "Slowdown and have a good plan" is an empowered idea and action.

On the other hand, if you have lots of great ideas, a sense of clarity and, you're ready to move on, but the fear that has accumulated along the way starts to creep in and tries to slow you down, just to feel safe, then "Slowdown and have a good plan" is not an empowered action. It is an excuse that may make you lose your divine timing and opportunities.

So you see, it is not the actual action, per se. It is the idea and the thoughts that powered the action. It is critical to know where this idea and these thoughts come from.

In my coaching, I often give my clients an emotional compass for them to monitor their emotion and record what emotion they feel the moment they have this idea or these thoughts. I divide the compass into two zones. The top is the empowered action-taking zone. The bottom part is the inner-work zone. So if your emotion is located in the empowered action-taking zone, then this idea and action is worth taking. Otherwise, you have to do some inner work to move your emotion into the empowered action-taking zone.

If you have any question or need further help, I can be reached at support@hoeholisticwellness.com.

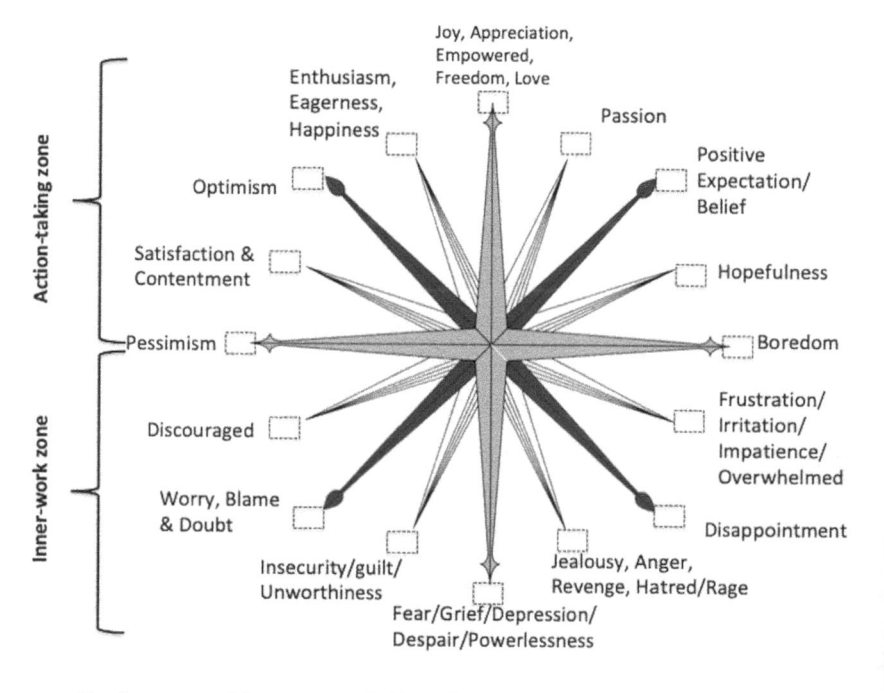

So by now, if you are following the steps, you have learned how to build momentum, when to take empowered action to help you move from idea to empowered action and into reality. Now you are ready to move on to the final step, build your blueprint, and road test your plan.

Notes

Chapter 10

Step 7: L for Level

(Level a New Career Path by Passing the Stress Test)

*"Not all storms come to disrupt your life;
some come to clear your path."*
– Unknown

What Will It Look Like After the Decision?

You made it to the last step of the process! Congratulations!

If you are following the instructions of each step, by now, you should know:

- What is your calling?
- What you don't want in your career?
- What you DO want exactly in your career?
- What is stopping, slowing you down or preventing you from moving forward?

Now it's time to lay out your plan and have a stress test.

The other day, my son installed a new liquid cooling system into his mega computer. He has been running big programs for 3D animation and his old cooling system could not keep up when his computer heated up to eighty-five degrees. After he installed his new cooling system, he told me he was going to run a stress test. I asked him, how was he going to do that. He told me he would run as many programs as possible to see how much the CPU (central processing unit) and GPU (graphic processing unit) would heat up. He showed me the heat sink, a thermally conductive metal piece placed over the CPU and the GPU to absorb some of the heat and pass the heat to the cooling system, where there is the fan and the liquid pipes. It was pretty cool.

That made me think of us, all the over-worked clinicians and scientists, how we're burnt-out by the heat we generate without having a good enough cooling system. No matter if you have decided to stay or leave your job, it is essential to upgrade your cooling system so that you will not burn out again. Think about all the scenarios that caused stress in your old career and test if they will also show up in your transition period and in your future career.

Stress Test Your Cooling System

Let's take another look at the list of stress factors mentioned in the National Physician Burnout, Depression & Suicide Report 2019 based on a survey of 15,069 physicians across 29 specialities. According to this report, the contributing factors of physician burnout include:

- Too many bureaucratic tasks (e.g. charting, paperwork)
- Spending too many hours at work
- Increasing computerization of practice

- Lack of respect from administrators/employers, colleagues, or staff
- Insufficient compensation/reimbursement
- Lack of control/autonomy
- Government regulations
- Feeling like just a cog in a machine
- Emphasis on profits over patients
- Lack of respect from patients
- Similar factors also contributing to the medical research scientists include:
- Too many bureaucratic tasks (e.g. grant applications, IACUC protocol, IBC protocol, IRB protocol, financial budgeting, personnel, and lab safety paperwork)
- Spending too many hours at work
- Long hours working on a computer
- Lack of respect from administrators/employers, colleagues, or staff
- Insufficient compensation/reimbursement
- Shortage of research funding
- Emphasis on translational aspect (e.g. if the research would lead to a profitable drug or treatment) and less emphasis on basic research and alternative healing
- Lack of respect from clinical hospital

According to this report, burnout affects many areas of our life in various ways including:

- Dreading coming to work
- Withered family relationships
- Rarely making plans to do anything socially as they are likely to be canceled

- Drinking more and less active
- Having many medical issues
- Lack of enthusiasm for patient care

More problems were created while coping with the burnout which include:

- Isolating yourself from others
- Wanting to sleep more when not working
- Eating junk food
- Drinking alcohol
- Binge eating
- Smoking cigarettes and other nicotine product
- Using prescription drugs
- Using marijuana products

To make matters worse, the report pointed out that the majority of physicians don't seek help. "Medical training teaches us to 'suck it up' so help-seeking is not a well-honed skill among doctors" and "Because the majority of doctors are overworked, exhausted and discontented, they've normalized their misery and pretend that it's not as bad as it seems."

The excuses of not getting help for their stress, depression, and other mental issues include:

- Symptoms are not severe enough
- I can deal with this without help from a professional
- Too busy
- Don't want to risk disclosure

Now, these factors summarize most of the stress that's found in the medical career. Let's test these out in your new career.

First, if you were in your bravest version of yourself, would you decide to stay in your current career or quit and move on to a new career?

If you decide to stay, what will you do differently? How will the above-mentioned stress factors be dealt with differently? Will you seek any help? What kind of help? How will that help you?

Road Test Checklist

If you decide to quit and move on to a different career, here is the checklist for you to make your plan:

1. Do you want to work for others or do you want to be your own boss as an entrepreneur?

	Find a New Job	Start a New Business
Pro		
Con		
Are these cons ok for me? If not, how I am going to deal with them?		

2. What area would you like to work? Make a list of all possible jobs and businesses that match what you worked out in chapters 4, 5, and 7.

	My Dream Career	What Job or Business May Match My Dream
Who do I want to serve and how am I good at serving these people?	Example: I want to help brilliant medical professionals who are thinking of quitting and I am good at coaching them how to quit and build their dream career of helping people live a heavenly life.	Example: Self-help book author, life coach, owner of a retreat center, online master class teacher, etc.
New work hours = actual hours of your current job – hours you need for self-care, family, vacation, etc.	Example: Work with my clients 3 days a week, business 2 days a week. Have uninterrupted weekends with family. A week of vacation and self-care every quarter of the year. No blackout on major holidays.	

How flexible are my working hours and working location?	Example: I can work with my clients from anywhere with flexible hours.	
How much does your new job/business earn? (E.g. Your hourly, monthly, or yearly salary or income)	Example: Double my current salary etc. Put in actual number so you will have a visual.	

3. How much time will you give yourself for the transition (from quitting your job to finding a new job or starting a new business)? Will you be able to give yourself a non-negotiable date? I call this date the sacred day of freedom (SDF). This will be the day when you have total clarity of your purpose, your mission, and your vision of what you want to achieve in the rest of your life. When you achieve this, you will have no regrets on your deathbed. And you are free from doubts, uncertainty, and fear. You are 100% living with unquestionable bravery. It feels like being brave enough to walk on the burning coals. It is a day that feels like rebirth, awakening, and empowerment. When my clients reach this status, I can feel their energy and light. They are radiant!

4. Will you need the supplement of passive income during the transition?

This is very critical and personal. This is what you should sit down with your spouse and work on together. Getting your family support and having your spouse on the same page as you to share your vision is a must. Here are examples of resources during the transition period:

- Continue your current job and getting paid. Slowly reduce your work hours from full-time to part-time. If you are already burnt-out from full-time working, it is impossible for you to have any energy to look for a new job or build your own business.
- Quit your job and live on your savings so you can go full-time and with full speed working on finding a new job or building your own business.
- Passive income resources:
  - Stocks
  - Cash back credit
  - Rental house
  - Join Getaround renting your unused car to others
  - If you drive a lot, you might want to use Wrapify to advertise other businesses on your car
  - Have an online blog and earn commission by promoting a product that's in alignment with your values through affiliate marketing
  - Create and sell an online course through platforms like YouTube, Udemy, Kajabi, etc.
  - If you love photography, you can sell your photos online
  - Fund your dream bank account, temporarily cut back the spending.

1. Do you need additional training?

If you decide to find another job, you have to think about what kind of job would let you have less stress but similar income as you are having now? Do you need more training for that specific job? If you decide to be an entrepreneur, are you prepared to handle the different types of challenges of managing a business? Do you need more training? How much time and money you want to invest?

2. Support, Support, Support

Who can understand your vision and purpose? Who can hold you accountable, and guide you through this transition period? Who will push you when you feel like falling back? Who will cheer you on when you are frustrated and feeling low on energy?

3. A Bridge Job That Is Less Draining

What kind of job is less demanding so that at the end of the day you will have energy, time, and mental space to build your new career?

4. Massive All-In Challenge

Set up a challenge with time, goal, coach or accountability partner.

For example, "I will quit my job by December 31, 2019. By that time, I will have my resignation letter submitted, a bridge job or six months of time funded by my "Fund my dream" bank account, to establish my new dream career. I will have my coach guide me through this process and hold me accountable if I am getting distracted, holding back, or behind schedule."

It is important to set the challenge and have an accountability partner because we are so easily distracted by so many things in life that are trying to get our attention every day. Once we get distracted we lose our momentum. When I wrote this book, I had the best book and life coach, Dr. Angela and her team, to hold me accountable every week to get the first book draft done in just nine weeks. Otherwise, this book may have taken me nine years or more to finish. Without the accountability partner, I am sure I would have found something in my life that would've convinced me to push this book project aside and wait. There would've been no momentum, no cohesive energy built into the book, and the message would've been lost.

The transition period is like another ten-month pregnancy of rebirth. Only this time, when you are born again, you won't need physical growth and survival. But just like learning physical survival skills, you will experience a personal growth and transformation. You may not need your biological family to nurture you this time. But you very much need a village, a tribe, a community where you feel you belong, and are safe, loved, and supported. And just like you need a mentor for your academy training, a good mentor is absolutely critical for this period of personal growth. Looking back throughout my life, I've truly enjoyed all my mentors. They are like my father, mother, or elder sisters and brothers. They appear at the right time and the right place for me to meet them. Each one supported me with exactly the help and guidance I needed at that period. I just can't imagine where I would be without them. Just because we graduated from medical schools doesn't mean we don't need help and mentorship anymore. On the contrary, if you are on this path of transformation, you would not be reading this book. There is so much on the path which we did not prepare for at medical school. So make a list of things you need help for and picture your next mentor here. The Universe will deliver you the opportunity.

	Things I Need Help For	What Types of Mentors I Would Like to Work With
Quitting My Current Job		
Getting My Family Support		
Find My Dream Job or Building My Dream Business		

Now you have a plan and passed your stress test. If you have any questions or would like me to work you through this, I can be reached at support@hoeholisticwellness.com.

Notes

Part 3

Proceed with Inevitable Success

Chapter 11

Why Most People Either Can't Make the Decision or Regret the Decision Later

The Story of Two Monks

Once upon a time, there were two monks who lived in the temples on top of two mountains. Every day they went down to the valley between the mountains to fetch water from the river. It was a tedious and exhausting task for both of them. They had to rest a long while before they would head back and they became good friends. One day, one of the monks didn't show up. Then another day went by and then weeks went by; he still didn't show up. The other monk started to wonder what happened to him. He decided to climb the other mountain to find out. When he finally found the temple, without address and GPS of course, he was surprised to see the other monk was not sick or anything. He asked him what happened all these days and how he could survive without water. That monk then brought him down to the vegetable garden of the temple and showed him a well that he had dug. Now he no longer needed to go down to the valley every day and he had more time to study and serve.

You are raised to believe in hard work and sacrifice, and you proudly build your medical career with honor, and you earn a high salary as compared to other jobs, only to become exhausted mentally and physically with not much of a family life. These conditions are something a lot of people would accept. Therefore, many don't even think about quitting.

But for those who have thought about it, if they could not see their future, where it is possible to have the honor to serve people, and at the same time, take care of themselves and have a family life, they would just take back the thought of quitting.

Then again, there will be a few really brave souls who dare to quit and find their way through trial and error. For them, that experience will likely come with hardship as they will suffer within their current career before figuring it all out.

My 7-step UPLEVEL process is designed to help people avoid these scenarios so that those who had the thought of quitting can do so and move on with their lives knowing these tools can help them build a regret-free plan.

Anyone can quit a job and find another one. Most of them are just going from one job to another to make a living. Maybe they will get a salary raise or a title promotion. Without the deep work described in these 7 steps, they will not find a true difference, true freedom, or true satisfaction and fulfillment.

Why Following the 7-Step UPLEVEL Process Is So Important?

Now let's take a look at how important this 7-step process is by examining what could happen if each step is not there to support your forward moving momentum.

Step 1: Unloading the Problem Is the Foundation

Remember, even when my son was told by his piano teacher that no matter how he performed in audition, he was already awarded. He was too young to understand this idea. He continued to panic and became frustrated. Later he had to quit piano to avoid going crazy.

Almost no one who is struggling with decision-making knows this step. Otherwise, they wouldn't be struggling. It is not easy to wrap our heads around the idea that the future is already existing and that you have choices each step of the way. Your NOW moment is the memory of the future you. Just take a moment to think about it. Once you can understand and accept this, your life will never be the same because you will be totally in charge. No more frustration and drama is needed. Without this step, you will be doing the guesswork and doubting yourself each step of the way, and giving up when things are not going your way or are slow to come.

I had a hard time watching my son suffer the stress and depression while I could not get my message through. But it is his path to walk. Some times a family member is not your best mentor even if the message is right. I am sure my son will get the message at the right time from the right person. The timing is important and the affinity is another factor. Therefore, getting help outside your usual family and friend circle is critical for making out-of-the box breakthroughs.

You're asking the question of quitting your medical career and you're reading this book for a reason. This might very well be your time and message. Remember, without Step 1, other steps will be shaky. So take the time to absorb this message. If you need me to help you practice this until it becomes your new foundation, you know how to reach me.

Step 2: Purpose (Reclaiming Your Purpose) Is the Pillar

Knowing what we really want is the pillar of creating your future career.

There were once two mice that fell into a big can of milk. One of the mice panicked and thought this was the end of his life. He was so sad that he was going to drown. The more he thought about it, the weaker he felt. Soon he drowned exactly as he thought he would. The other mouse kept swimming and thinking that he was going to get out of the can. Every stroke made him feel he was getting closer. He pictured himself rising higher and higher and then he could just jump out of the can very soon. He thought of his family waiting for him and he could almost see them hugging him and licking the milk off of him. He kept swimming and swimming. Soon the milk started to solidify and he was able to lift himself out of the can.

Only when we are clear about what we really want can we bring that thing into our reality. Without Step 2, we will not be able to shift our attention from things we don't want to things we truly want. Without Step 2, we will not be able to appreciate how all the things we don't like are what's actually helping us to know what we want to be better. Without Step 2, we will continue to struggle and suffer even if we quit and find another job.

Step 3: Leverage (Turning Quitting into Upgrading) Is the Game Changer

Looking at quitting from a different perspective is the game changer.

There was this monkey trainer who tried to feed monkeys twice a day. He had seven peaches for each monkey. He told the monkeys that they could only have three in the morning and four in the afternoon. The monkeys were not happy. They all jumped up screaming to protest and ask for more peaches. The monkey trainer shook his head reluctantly and said, "All right, all right, you win. You will all have four peaches in the morning and three in the afternoon." The monkeys were all happy and started to quiet down.

When you want to quit your medical career, you have your inner monkeys that are not going to be happy with the word "quit" and the stigma that comes with it. These monkeys were raised in the culture of "never quit," hard work, and "sacrifice." They will be sure to protest. This will for sure put you in a hard position when family and friends have concerns with your decision and their words may resonate with your inner monkeys. When that happens, it will successfully drag you back to that same unhappy place. Therefore, it is so important to convince your inner monkeys first that you are not quitting. You are upgrading and they all get promotions in the new career. You will work more efficiently and help more people in the best version of yourself.

Only after you quiet down your inner monkeys can you start to have clarity on what you want for your new career.

Step 4: Envision (Building Your Unique Vision, and Saying, "Yes, I Am Coming.") Is the Core Wisdom

Build the vision is the core wisdom.

Most people, especially medical professionals, spend their busy days on autopilot and have no time left to create a vision. Where you look is where you drive. Without Step 4, you will keep driving into the same old burnt-out situations. You will be surrounded by people who are exhausted and getting into medical accidents, etc. If you want to work in a different environment, you have to take time to draw the blueprint. And nothing could compare to the beauty of borrowing wisdom from the future you. You don't have to wait. You can embody that wisdom now with Step 4.

Step 5: Voice (Removing Roadblocks and Internal Conflicts) Is the Key for Inevitable Success

Removing inner conflict is the key to inevitable success.

Internal conflict is the root of all chronic health issues, which are literally spelled Dis-Ease. Any decision made without easing the dis-ease will only be heading backward in no time. Therefore, Step 5 is the essential peacemaker that will untangle the dis-ease and not only make peace but also create new solutions that all parts will be rejoiced. The step paves the path of inevitable success.

Step 6: Empower (Taking Only Empowered Action) Is the Momentum

Taking only empowered action is the key to power the momentum.

As we discussed before, without momentum, matters will remain in the original place. Same as your career upgrading. Step 6 not only gives you tools to build the momentum. It also gives you tools to identify the direction of the momentum. Without Step 6, you either get stuck at where you are, or you may be pulled back in the wrong direction. Remember Gravity

1 is your enemy and Gravity 2 is your friend. If mixed up, your career would go backwards.

Step 7: Leveling the New Path (Planning a New Career That Can Pass the Stress Test) Is the Quality Control

The stress test is the quality control for your blueprint.

It takes practice to change our habitual thinking. Knowing what we should do doesn't ensure follow up action. By the end of Step 6, we should have setup conditions that will lead us to inevitable success. That means we will know exactly what to do when old habits comes up to challenge new habits. The stress test is to check if our conditions are set correctly so that we will not fall back into the old habit. Take hiking in the forest for example. There are trails you have walked on many times. There are trails hardly walked on. When you are given the choice at a crossroads, it is almost a no-brainer to choose to walk on the old path that is paved. So setting up an inevitable condition keeps us focused on the new path, for example your newly planned career path, without getting distracted or tempered by the old career path. The stress test puts you at the crossroads to see if you can still take the new career path. Without the stress test, you would not know if your blueprint would work. Most people build their blueprint out of fear and this is when you will make a decision that you will regret.

Warning: Things may get worse before they get better

I have a wonderful archery coach, Tom Herrington, who often warns team members, "Your score will actually get worse when we start to improve your form." It may sound strange.

But we, again and again, experience that strange phenomenon. This phenomenon is not just happening to athletes. It actually happens to most clients coached by master coaches before their lives are transformed into their desired lives. Whether it is weight loss, relationship, career, or finance, etc. Understanding this phenomenon is critical to not doubting the decision you made when you are actually on the right track.

Now why do things often get worse before they get better?

Our autopilot life and our old habits have established the framework of our life. Our career is a huge piece of that structure. Quitting a medical career will certainly shake up that structure. There will be many moving parts that will no longer be in the old positions and there will be temporary break downs, break ups and break throughs. In addition to our career, our relationships, family, and finance will all be affected. But these being out of position are temporarily for the better alignment later.

- You may experience a financial setback
- You relationship may be put to test;
- You may lose a friendship;
- You may be misunderstood by your parents, spouse, or children...

When these things happen, don't think that you made a wrong decision.

These are just like sands in a water bottle. The stir-ups will never last. Once settled, the clear water is what will last. Soon, you will find:

You are earning the same amount of money or even more than your old career;

Your relationships will get stronger after the test of your career transition;

If someone has to exit your life, this might be the best time;

You can allow people to be where they are while you move on;

When you are back on your feet, happy and healthy, your new life speaks a thousand words in your defense. All those who were against you will envy you.

Move forward, my friend. Do not fear! Fear actually has many names and none of which is really about fear:

False **E**vidence **A**ppearing **R**eal
Face **E**verything **A**nd **R**ise
Feel **E**xcited **A**nd **R**eady

Which one is yours?

One way to sustain fear is having neither a plan nor clarity around your options. So follow the UPLEVEL to make your plan and list all your options and then you will upgrade your medical career in no time. It's time to move on with your life and I will always be here to answer any questions and provide a helping hand!

Notes

Chapter 12

What Is Your Life Mission Statement?

"Fear is you imagining the worst.
Faith is you imagining a higher purpose."
– Tony Robbins

What Is Your Higher Purpose?

t is no accident you asked the question at this moment in life. It is no accident you are reading this book. Crossroads are opportunities to breakthrough and upgrade.

I hope after reading this 7-step process, your life will no longer be the same. Regardless if the decision you reached is to stay or to leave, if you follow these 7 steps, your life experience will be upgraded. You will either move forward to a different career or move forward to the next level of success in your current job. This process not only helps you to make your decision, more importantly, it helps you to succeed no matter your decision because our life is composed of a series of decision-making events. This 7-step process can be applied to any decision-making issue in your life.

But before you close the book, there is one thing I want you to write down, frame, and display somewhere in your office or bedroom etc. so that it can remind you why you are here. You guessed it right. It is your life mission statement. In the statement, you can describe who you want to serve. In what way? What do you need to achieve in this life so that when you leave you will be at peace and you know you didn't waste all your time here?

The Story of Bian Que and His Two Physician Brothers

Bian Que is the earliest known Chinese physician. Once the king of the country Wei asked him: "I heard you have two brothers who are also practicing medicine. Which one of you is the best?" Bian replied, "My older brother is the best, my middle brother is the second, and I am the worst." The king was surprised. "So why are you the most famous one?"

Bian replied, "My older brother cures his patient before the onset of any symptoms. Because most people do not know that he helped them eradicate the cause of their disease before the patient even knew they had any problems, people think he is a fraud. His fame is only within the family, as only we know he is the best doctor. My middle brother is treating the disease at the beginning of the illness, the average person thinks that he can only cure minor illnesses, so his fame is only in his hometown. I don't have my brother's skill. I only treat patients when they are at the most severe stage. People see me using an acupuncture needle on the meridians to bleed and apply strong toxic medicine on the skin. They thought that my skills were so great. That's why my reputation was heard throughout the country."

To know your mission, you have to know who you want to serve and what problem you would like to help them to solve. Many people think treating cancer patients, preventing pandemic spreading of Ebola, saving emergency patients, performing heart or brain surgeries are super heroic and technically challenging. Yes, there are so many patients out there needing modern medicine. However, not many would appreciate the challenge to coach people for habit changes when their lives still seem perfect and there is no sign of symptoms on the horizon.

Equipped with the best medicine technique at his time, even Bian Que could not take this challenge. Legend tells that once when Bian Que was traveling passing the state of Cai, he met the lord of the state and just by observing him he knew that he was incubating a disease. Bian told the lord but said that the illness was only in his skin. The lord laughed at this, and told his attendants that Bian Que was just trying to profit from the fears of people. He must be a fraud. Bian was reluctant but tried to visit the lord many times thereafter, alerting him each time how this sickness was progressing from his skin to his blood and to his organs. During his last visit, Bian saw the lord before and saw him up close, then immediately ran out of the palace. When people asked him why he had to run away, he told them that the disease had spread into the marrow and was incurable. Soon the lord would ask him to treat him. He would be killed if he could not cure him. The lord died soon after Bian Que's last visit.

No wonder, Bian Que admired his brothers who could treat people before the onset of any symptoms and not be given any credit for their health and happiness. To Bian Que, they were the real heroes and possessed real wisdom. It also looked like Bian Que's brothers lived a better life than him. They lived in their villages with an easy-going lifestyle although it was without fame. Whereas Bian Que was busy traveling and treating VIP patients like the kings and the lords. Famous and well-respected, but busy and risky.

This is your opportunity to re-examine your servant's heart and ask the question, for the rest of your life, who would you like to serve in your new career. People who are deep into their illness, people who are just starting to show mild symptoms, or people who do not have any symptoms yet but are willing to make a habit change so they don't have to experience illness down the road. Or you could totally change the field. A friend of mine quit her medical research professor job and started her own company to help researchers and clinical staffs with their scientific writing and editing for publishing or grant application. You see, who you serve will define your career path. Once you've identified who you would like to serve the most, you can proceed to write your mission statement. Make sure you state why and how you would like to serve these people, and what you would like to do to serve.

My Mission Is to Support Your Mission

When I was young, career to me only meant a job that gave you a paycheck so you could live a life. It was an exchange of labor or intelligent work like my parents did. I never thought of serving anyone or fulfilling some life purpose or having a mission through my career.

After years of doing research under tight funding, I grew tired of spending my best years buried in paperwork, chasing research funding, and publishing research papers solely for the purpose of getting my research funded. It was a brutal "publish or perish" world. I am also tired of talking to biotech and pharmaceutical industry investors, whose interest will dangerously deviate from the true purpose of my research. After witnessing the unbearable loss of my mentor and seeing how exhausted my medical oncology colleagues were in our hospital, I knew that continuing on this career path was no longer a choice for me. This is an individual choice.

There have to be other ways to help people without killing ourselves!

You know you are intelligent, gifted, hardworking, and have the servant's heart to save lives. Who could be in a better position to shoulder the task to turn this Earth into heaven? And yet, you are burnt-out, overwhelmed, and not the best version of yourself. Being in one of the least healthy professions, which ironically was designed to take care of other people's health issues, you thought about quitting but were not sure where to go. It breaks my heart to see you – who have the most potential to change the world into a happier and healthier place – suffering and unable to do what you are meant to do.

I could not be happier to have this book and my coaching program, Fellowship of HOpE, to help you get back to your feet, reconnect to your purpose, and rediscover a better career path so that you can live a satisfactorily fulfilling life where you can save lives in a better way and still have time for self-care and quality family time.

No more sacrifices to your health and wellness to save others. Sacrifice is a word in the right column of the right-or-wrong table. It sounds right. But it doesn't feel good and more importantly is not sustainable. It is this very mindset that got you burnt-out and unable to model a healthy life for others who look up to you for guidance. It's time to ditch that mindset and ask, "What if I can help other people more with their life without sacrificing mine?"

Humans are more intelligent and have stronger free wills than any other species on earth. And yet, we are the only species that does not rely on self-healing. Before we figure out the ultimate game of self-healing, all types of physicians, therapists, healers, and coaches help people at different stages of awakening. You might very well be here at this time of your life for a new movement: Turn disease-care into healthcare in your current position or in a new career outside current medical system.

This book and The Fellowship of HOpE program are designed to help the transition of any medical professionals who would like to upgrade their game.

What is your life mission statement?

Send me your mission statement at support@hoeholisticwellness. com. I am eager to discuss and support you with your unique mission!

Notes

_____

_____

_____

_____

_____

_____

_____

_____

_____

_____

_____

_____

_____

_____

_____

_____

_____

_____

Afterword

A few years after our Vermont trip to the Big Maze, I found another type of maze, the labyrinth. A modern-day labyrinth may look like a maze at first glance. But it has a significant difference if you look closely. The traditional maze is a complex puzzle designed to challenge you with branching paths and different choices of entrances, directions, dead ends, and exits. A maze can get you frustrated, frightened, exhausted, and you can get lost in it. Labyrinths, on the other hand, have a single, non-branching path that leads you to the center destination and back. There are still twists and turns. But there is no way for you to get lost. Instead of feeling frustrated and challenged, you will feel peace and joy in the labyrinth. I really fell in love with this type of maze. I also obtained a mini-sand labyrinth for meditation.

It is my hope that this book will bring you peace, joy, and inspiration during your transition from the medical career maze to a future career of a labyrinth.

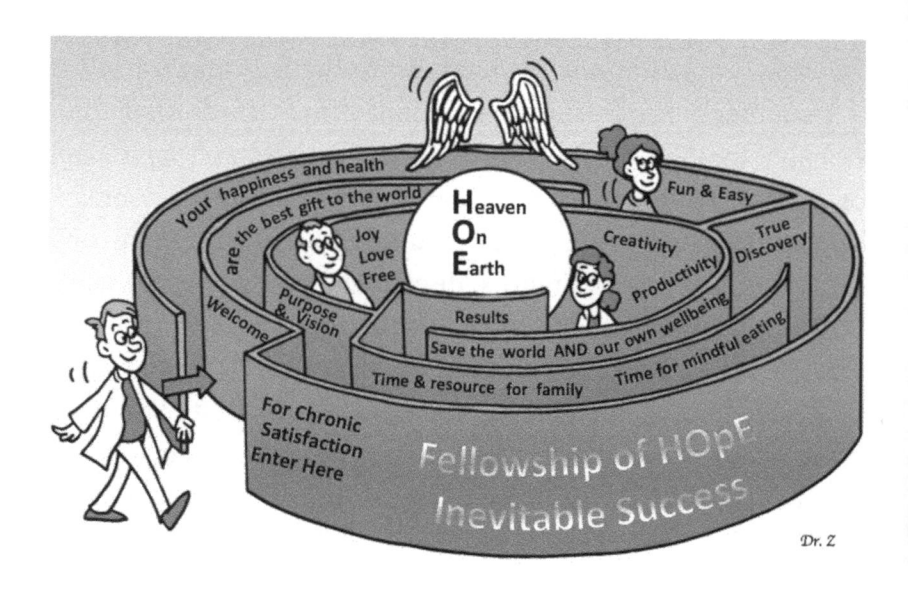

Acknowledgements

To me, spending ten months making a human being is not a miracle. I did it twice. But I never thought I could write a book in nine weeks. Words cannot express my gratitude towards Dr. Angela Lauria and her team at The Author Incubator who made this nine-week journey a life-changing miracle for me.

This book would not be possible without all the former medical school students, physicians, nurses, and therapists who quit their medical career and inspired me and allowed me to work with them and interview them. The understanding, support, and appreciation from my research lab members and students were my inspiration to transition out of my medical career and to become a life coach.

I would not have become a master level coach without the training at Health Coach Institute. I learned to be authentic and feel comfortable to be vulnerable from Carey Peters; I learned to soften and coach in the flow from Stacey Morgenstern; I learned to coach and build a business with compassion from Bill Baren. My mentors, coaches, and the coach tribe are what kept me going.

I also want to thank my friends who gave me the best teas and Zen fountains to make my long hours of writing pleasant.

Thank you to Angela Lauria and The Author Incubator's team, as well as to David Hancock and the Morgan James Publishing team for helping me bring this book to print.

Last but not least, I'd like to thank my family. Without the understanding and support of my husband and my children, you would not be reading this book.

Thank You for Reading My Book

I know this may sound weird. Before you read this book, you had already participated in the creation of this book. Know that in your search for an answer to your question, "Should I quit my medical career or not?", the Universe is answering. In my own struggle and the journey toward my own calling, our paths crossed. And so many people had to ask and so many life events had to happen before the realization of this book.

Please accept a small token from me, my dear reader, for helping me to create this book, I designed you a gift from the Fellowship of HOpE. Please email me your shipping address so I can send it to you.

Xuemei Zhong, Ph.D. marks her debut in the publishing world with the release of "The Traveler" (initially published by Balboa Press). This new book is a modern-day parable that encourages readers to seek the essential truths in the midst of the vicissitudes of life.

After her debut book, The Traveler Book 1, Dr. Xuemei Zhong continued the journey of the traveler. But this time, the story follows a flock of geese. Zacarias is a young goose in a flock where everyone strictly follows tradition and rules. When her gut feeling tells her something needs to be changed, she ventures to propose a new way of flying during the seasonal migration. Will her proposal be accepted or will she be questioned?

About the Author

Dr. Xuemei Zhong went through a journey from a medical school professor to becoming a life coach, author, and speaker. Early in her medical profession, she had a passion for transforming disease-care to true health and self-care. Dr. Zhong received her PhD in immunology and pathology. Her own Immuno-Oncology research and life experience revealed to her that our bodies are our best doctors. The irony of medical professionals being one of the least healthy populations drove her to look for a better career choice and to help like-minded medical professionals find their dream career – that both aligns with their purpose but also helps them sustain a healthy lifestyle. She finally felt at home when she received training and became certified health coach and master level transformational life coach. Through her journey of leaving a traditional medical career and establishing her own coaching business, she witnessed so many hardships and struggles that she was determined to work with those incredibly smart medical professionals who did not feel fulfilled and did not want to spend the rest of their careers physically and mentally exhausted. Dr. Zhong coaches them on how to quit and create a fulfilling new career. Dr. Zhong founded the HOE Holistic Wellness LLC. The motto of her business is "Stop hoping, start be-living." She believes that "when we take the "P" (things that prevent people from their dream life) out of HOPE it becomes HOE (Heaven on Earth)." Dr. Zhong created "The Fellowship of HOpE" program to coach medical professionals to create a new career that is in better alignment with their calling and dream. She believes that medical professionals who have a dream bigger than their current practice are going to have a big impact in transforming human life into a heavenly experience.

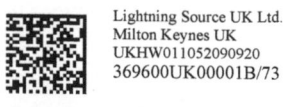

9 781642 798821